CLASSIC

BRITISH
MOTORCYCLES

COLIN JACKSON

FONTHILL

FONTHILL MEDIA
www.fonthillmedia.com

A CIP catalogue record for this book is available from the British Library

Typeset in 10pt on 12pt Sabon LT Std
Typesetting by Fonthill Media
Printed in the UK

ISBN 978-1-78155-431-9

Contents

Acknowledgements

Thank you to Tony East (proprietor of the A.R.E. motorcycle museum in Kirk Michael), Job Grimshaw, Bob Taylor aka 'Wobbly Bob', Bill Bewley, Richard Blackburn, Guenter Kranz, Adrian Pingstone, Ronald Jennings, Robin Vincent-Day, Paul D'Orleans (aka The Vintagent), Ron Coombs and all those others who have read through the manuscript and provided information, anecdotes and coffee.

For detailed information on classic motorcycles see: *crazyguyonabike.com* (article by Carsten Hoefer: 'A Short Illustrated History of the Bicycle'); *Vintage Mann* (the official journal of the Isle of Man section VMCC); Grace's online Guide to British Industrial History (F. E. Baker Ltd, Villiers engines, Minerva engines and many of the reproductions of early twentieth-century advertising); and www.cybermotorcycle.com, which contains a wealth of information for the classic motorcycle enthusiast.

Any errors you find are of course my own.

Introduction

Today, the motorcycle is a familiar sight in many forms. It ranges from the low-powered pizza delivery moped, to scooters, small commuter bikes, powerful sports machines, tourers, all the way to MotoGP racers. In London you can hire a motorcycle taxi to whisk you through the capital's traffic. Should you happen to die in County Down, Northern Ireland, you can even travel to the cemetery in a hearse pulled by a motorcycle.

A few of today's most popular bikes, mainly top-end models such as Ducati and Aprilia, come from Italy, but the majority are Japanese, with the 'big four' companies – Honda, Suzuki, Yamaha and Kawasaki – dominating the market. But it has not always been this way. For much of the twentieth century, British-made motorbikes ruled supreme, and (mostly) British designers and engineers made that possible.

During the First World War, many young men were introduced to motorised transport by the military; on their return home they discovered a world that was rapidly changing. It was a world in which the car and the motorcycle were replacing the horse and carriage, and of the two, motorcycles were definitely the way to go if you wanted to cut a bit of a dash. It has been said that motorcycles such as the Brough Superior, the Matchless and the Douglas racing at Brooklands, Pendine and the Isle of Man really put the roar into the Roaring Twenties.

Such bikes laid the foundation of British dominance in the motorcycling world, which would last for many decades. This is the story of that golden age. This book is an attempt to trace the evolution of the motorcycle from its earliest, oiliest, most unreliable simplicity to the vastly more developed forms we see today. The focus is firmly on the contributions made by British engineers, companies and individuals, but there may be a few surprises along the way; not everything is quite as British as we may like to think.

The story does not have a clear beginning. The bicycle could be considered as a starting point perhaps, but then this piece of engineering could be traced back to the invention of the wheel. Therefore, let us start with what was effectively the re-invention of the wheel by the English scientist/engineer, Sir George Cayley.

Sir George Cayley, 6th Baronet of Brompton, (1773-1857) was the first to identify the four forces of flight: lift, drag, thrust and weight. He built a successful manned glider and is sometimes referred to as the father of aerodynamics. He was also the inventor of the tension-spoked wheel. He realised in 1808 that a wheel in which the forces were absorbed through tension rather then compression could be made lighter, and that this would be an advantage when building an aircraft undercarriage. Cayley strung his wheels with 'tight cording', which was improved upon in 1849 by the use of wire spokes by another Englishman, George Stanley.

James Starley and William Hillman used wire spokes on their Ariel bicycles from 1870, and they were used on virtually all motorcycles until the arrival of cast alloy wheels in the 1970s. They are used today on bikes such as the current Triumph Thruxton.

The history of the bicycle itself is usually considered to begin with the arrival of the 'running machine' in 1817. The prolific German inventor Baron Karl von Drais realised that horses were an expensive form of transport requiring stabling, grooming and large quantities of food. He felt that a muscle-powered solution was desirable which would allow large numbers of people to travel faster than was possible by using legs alone.

Drais devised and built a machine with two wooden wheels in a wooden frame, fitted with a leather seat and a primitive handlebar to steer it. Aided by well-publicised rides made by Drais himself to demonstrate its usefulness (including one of 60 kilometres in only four hours), the running machine was a rapid success under various names in many countries. In its German home it was the Draisine, in France the Velocipede and in England the Hobby Horse (or Dandy Horse, reflecting a feeling that it was mostly popular with wealthy young men of the upper classes). As with many new ideas, the significance of the Draisine was not appreciated by all. One American writer commented, 'Every species of transatlantic nonsense, it would seem, is capable of exciting curiosity, no matter how ridiculous'.

The Draisine never made Drais much money since the patenting of inventions was still an idea for the future. In any case, the machine's popularity was short-lived. Apart from the difficulty of riding such a heavy machine, collisions with pedestrians led to it being banned in many places on both sides of the Atlantic.

The arrival of pedals cannot be dated with certainty. It is known that a Frenchman, Pierre Lallement, patented such a feature in 1866 in the USA but the design itself predated the patent and there are also several other potential claims to the title of 'first pedal-powered bicycle'. All have their adherents but none can be conclusively proved.

Initially the pedals were mounted directly to the front wheel, which inevitably resulted in the machine travelling only a short distance for each turn, effectively a 'low' gearing. Using a large front wheel solved this shortcoming, but at the expense of safety. These 'penny farthing' machines gave the rider a long way to fall.

A French watchmaker by the name of Andre Guilmet came up with the idea of using a chain to drive the rear wheel some time prior to 1870, but such was the popularity of the penny farthing (or more correctly the 'high wheeler') that early 'safety bicycles' actually used the chain to drive an only slightly smaller *front* wheel. The first recognisably modern bicycle did not appear until J. K. Starley introduced his 'dwarf safety', known as the Rover 2, in 1885. The Rover even had a chassis that looked much like the modern diamond frame.

> When man invented the bicycle he reached the peak of his attainments. Here was a machine of precision and balance for the convenience of man. And (unlike subsequent inventions for man's convenience) the more he used it, the fitter his body became. Here, for once, was a product of man's brain that was entirely beneficial to those who used it, and of no harm or irritation to others. Progress should have stopped when man invented the bicycle.
>
> – Elizabeth West, *Hovel in the Hills*

This author is prepared to admit that it is difficult to argue with the above, except in so far as pedestrians *were* injured by velocipedes even before pedals had been added, but it almost seems churlish to mention that. However, since this is a history of the motorcycle, we'll have to ignore what possibly ought to have been, and add an engine …

'Starley's Eye Opener'. (*Courtesy of Grace's Guide*)

Chapter 1

Early Experiments and Influential Engines

It was clear by the end of the nineteenth century that far greater distances could be covered with far greater ease if the cycle was fitted with an engine. We might assume that this meant an internal combustion engine, but no; the earliest motorcycle pioneers did not wait for this. There were a few brave souls who used external combustion – steam – engines to save their legs and increase their speed over the earth.

One such person was Sylvester Howard Roper, the son of a cabinetmaker, born in Francestown, New Hampshire, in 1823. Roper's interest in steam power was evident from a young age; he is thought to have built his first stationary engine when he was twelve and before he had actually seen one 'in the metal'. By 14 years old, and still before he saw anyone else's engines working, he had also made a locomotive engine. He was no mere tinkerer either. He developed impressive steam carriages, or 'buggies', which he was seen to drive around Boston in the 1860s, and also held patents for a new type of padlock and an improved knitting machine before getting a job with the Springfield Armoury during the American Civil War. His work on improving revolvers and shotguns would lead to further patents filed after the war, and there was also a fire escape reel designed to allow a fully controlled descent from a high building.

Roper's steam-powered velocipede, or motorbike, was reported to be capable of 40 mph and was publically advertised as being able to outrun a trotting horse. Sadly, it may be that Mr Roper was also the first to die in a motorcycle accident. The *Boston Globe* reported on 2 June 1896 that Sylvester H. Roper had 'died in the saddle'. He had previously been travelling at an impressive speed on the Charles River Park cycle track near Cambridge, Massachusetts, when he shut off the steam 'as if on premonition of the end' and fell from the machine. The doctor's report stated that he had sustained a head wound, but that the actual cause of death was heart failure. He was unable to say whether Roper's heart had failed as a result of the crash or had been the cause of it. Shutting off the steam in advance of his fall might perhaps suggest the latter. It is easy to imagine that riding a steam-powered bicycle at 40 mph on a cycle track at the age of 72 could have been stressful enough to cause a heart attack.

Roper must have been fairly well known, at least in the Boston area, as the report of his death appears to have made the front page. His machine can be seen at the Smithsonian Institute.

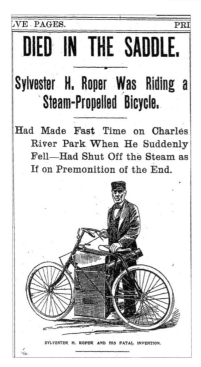

VE PAGES.   PRI

DIED IN THE SADDLE.

Sylvester H. Roper Was Riding a Steam-Propelled Bicycle.

Had Made Fast Time on Charles River Park When He Suddenly Fell—Had Shut Off the Steam as If on Premonition of the End.

SYLVESTER H. ROPER AND HIS FATAL INVENTION.

Was Sylvester H. Roper the first motorcycle fatality? The machine itself is now kept in the Smithsonian Institution. (Boston Daily Globe, *2 June 1896*)

Despite the best efforts of Roper and of one or two others in various parts of the world, steam power was never a truly practical solution for a powered bicycle, and so the development of small and reasonably efficient liquid-fuelled *internal* combustion engines was the real key to progress.

As hinted at previously, cycles did not only have two wheels at this time. When engines were introduced there were three wheelers (tricycles) and four wheelers (quadricycles) too, so the car and the motorbike can be regarded as branches of the same machine. Both also really got going in roughly the same place – not America or Britain, but Germany.

Gottlieb Daimler is generally credited with building the first 'true' motorcycle in around 1885. It had two wheels, positioned one behind the other, with a spring-loaded stabiliser wheel on each side. The machine, which was powered by a single-cylinder 264cc Otto-cycle engine, was constructed mostly of wood. Daimler's assistant, Wilhelm Maybach, was working on a spray carburettor, and this may have been fitted. The Daimler 'bike' is likely to have been capable of about 7 mph.

The first motorbike to be put into series production is generally accepted to have been the Hildebrand and Wolfmuller of 1894. Several hundred of these are thought to have been built over a three- or four-year period and a handful survive today. The water-cooled twin-cylinder four-stroke 1,489cc bike looks remarkably well-made compared to some other early motorcycles and could (indeed still can) cruise at about 30 mph.

The H&W's two large pistons are connected to a crank on the wheel spindle and the rear wheel doubles as a flywheel, so that in effect the rear of the bike is all part

The Cyclemaster engine dates from the 1950s but it illustrates a much earlier idea, allowing an engine to be added to a standard bicycle without additional modifications.

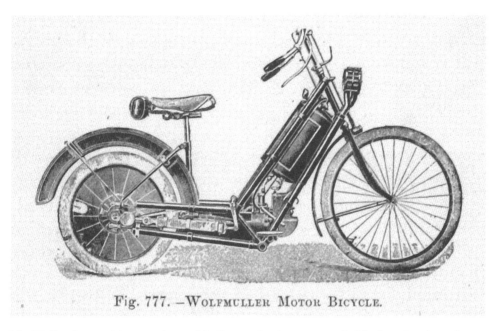

Fig. 777. —WOLFMULLER MOTOR BICYCLE.

The Wolfmuller machine was the world's first production motorcycle. The large 'mudguard' over the rear wheel is actually the water tank for the cooling system. (*Courtesy of Grace's Guide*)

of the engine. From the front, the overall appearance is of a powered bicycle, while from the side it is reminiscent of a steam locomotive because of the visible connecting rods.

The machine was expensive to produce and as it clearly could not stand still with the engine running it was quickly left behind by the rapid progress of technology, but it unquestionably represents one of the first big steps towards the modern motorcycle.

British engineers were certainly not idle during the initial stages of the motorcycle's development. Cycling was hugely popular in this country and Britain is a hilly place. There was plenty of incentive to put an engine into a bicycle.

In the early days, engineers, some trained, many others working in garden shed workshops, tended to start from the bicycle frame and general layout, while adding an engine to either supplement or replace the pedals. Various engine positions were tried, such as the centre of the rear wheel, above the front wheel and under the seat, but fairly quickly the engine settled in the bottom bracket, just where the cyclist's pedals had been.

However, with the removal of the requirement for muscle power, cars rapidly developed bodywork and effectively became powered carriages while the bicycle remained closer to its original form and became the motorcycle. It follows that the motorcycle was inherently cheaper and easier to produce and could remain within the reach of the mass market.

Many small firms with even quite basic engineering facilities soon turned their hands to powered bicycles. Many, but by no means all, were already in the bicycle business and bought in suitable engines from separate suppliers – and many of these were involved in building either cars or motorcycles themselves. Hence their stories became interwoven and potentially confusing. For example, Minerva engines were made in Antwerp, Belgium, and fitted to their own vehicles, but they were also sold to a number of early British motorcycle manufacturers.

A British firm by the name of 'Precision' produced motorcycles in the very early years of the twentieth century and these were fitted with Minerva engines. However, Frank Baker of Kings Norton, Birmingham, established the entirely separate 'Precision' company in 1906 to supply parts for bicycles. He designed and made his own engines and from 1912 was building complete motorcycles. By 1911, Precision engines were to be found powering almost a hundred motorcycle models from a large number of different manufacturers.

In 1919, following a gap in motorcycle production due to the First World War, the Precision Company merged with William Beardmore and Company, a Scottish engineering concern, and began to produce 'Beardmore Precision Motorcycles'. Then in 1924 Beardmore withdrew its capital and Baker set up his own new company but the machines now used Villiers engines!† The company was later sold to the James cycle company and Baker was employed as a designer. However, most James motorcycles used either Villiers or AMC engines.

---

† Villiers gained its name from its address on Villiers Street, Wolverhampton.

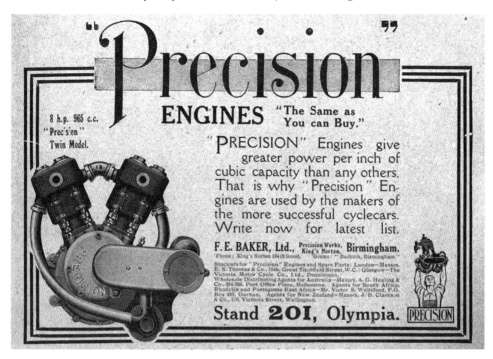

Advert for 'Precision' engines. (*Courtesy of Grace's Guide*)

Advert for JAP. (*Courtesy of Grace's Guide*)

J. A. Prestwich was another prodigious producer of engines. Theirs carried the 'JAP' name and were used by motorcycle builders large and small. Many of these have either gone out of business or been absorbed into larger conglomerates and their names have been forgotten, but the JAP name remains; it is associated with machines that even include the 'Rolls Royce of motorcycles', the Brough Superior.

An article in *MCN* on 7 May 2009 states that Prestwich supplied the engines for no fewer than 137 different machines. JAP engines even found their way into racing cars. The Cooper-JAP was enormously successful in both 500cc and 1,000/1,100cc forms from its introduction in 1946 right through to the end of the 1950s. Drivers who drove them (or even started their careers in them) included Stirling Moss, Peter Collins, Les Leston, Ken Tyrell, Graham Hill and even Bernie Ecclestone. Of course, the tradition of fitting motorcycle engines into small, lightweight track cars continues to the present day.

This page and opposite above: The Calthorpe Junior of 1914. Essentially a bicycle with a 'Precision' engine added. Note the early 'girder' front suspension, belt drive and bicycle brakes (although the rear blocks are greatly enlarged and act on the drive pulley rather than the wheel rim). The leather drive belt is removed from the pulley when not in use to prolong its life.

Below: JAP-engined Rotrax Speedway bike. (*Courtesy of P. Jahr*)

As the early motorcycle engines rapidly became more powerful so motorcycle speeds increased and it followed that the rest of the bike needed to improve too. A basic diamond-shaped bicycle frame was adequate at bicycle speeds but if such a machine hit a bump in the road at a much higher speed (and remember there were very few remotely smooth roads at the time) the entire machine would leave the ground. This was clearly dangerous and it was not long before attempts were made to improve things. Bikes such as the Calthorpe Junior had an early front suspension system which can be seen in the photographs. This takes the form of a basic girder fork, which is to say the entire front wheel and fork can move up and down on a set of linkages at the top. The linkages form an approximate parallelogram, enabling the 'girder' to move vertically. The spring then compresses to absorb the bump and return the wheel to its original position.

There is no damping on this bike. The fork (and indeed the rest of the bike) are free to bounce up and down after each bump, but it still represents an improvement over the solid frame. Damping came later, as did rear suspension, unless you count sprung saddles which were obviously only intended to improve rider comfort and did not benefit the handling of the machine.

Edward Turner (of Triumph Speed Twin and Ariel Square Four fame) designed a 'sprung hub' in 1938. This had the advantage that it could be fitted to a rigid frame without modification, but also the disadvantages that it allowed only 2 inches of travel and did not permit damping. The hub's development was delayed by the Second World War and it finally appeared on Ernie Lyons' specially prepared Triumph Tiger 100 in time for the 1946 Senior Manx Grand Prix. Lyons won the race in terrible weather conditions.

Surprisingly, both 'plunger' designs and modern-type swinging arms (sometimes called pivoted forks) arrived on a few machines even before the First World War. There are still machines (particularly American designs) on sale with solid rear ends to this day.

In the plunger suspension, the wheel moves vertically on two telescopic tubes containing coil springs. The swinging arm may use two coil spring/damper units placed on either side or a single one placed centrally and operated by linkages or cantilevers. This latter approach can give a reduction in unsprung mass (that part of the bike which is intended to follow the bumps) and assist the suspension in its job of keeping the wheel on the ground.

Calthorpe were just one of a host of motorcycle companies established in the late nineteenth or very early twentieth century. Many were eventually bought out and became part of the more famous firms while others simply went out of business; but many contributed ideas and engineering breakthroughs for which they are not generally credited today. Calthorpe's origins as a bicycle manufacturer are clearly visible in the 'Junior' and this again was entirely typical.

George Hands established the company in Birmingham in the last years of the nineteenth century, diversifying from bicycles into cars from 1904 and motorcycles after 1909. The 'Junior' model dates from the time of the First World War. It has a single-cylinder air-cooled four-stroke 'Precision' engine. Other Calthorpes were powered by JAP, Villiers, Peco and Blackburne. The Junior has a two-speed gearbox and a leather belt to drive the rear wheel. Note that the brakes are simple rubber blocks operated by cables – exactly as on bicycles – although the rear brake acts on the inner surface of the drive pulley.

Calthorpe were in fact one of the longer-lived manufacturers, having gone on to produce their own engines from 1924. The company survived until the start of the Second World War, at which time they were producing both solo and sidecar machines of advanced design. Their 'Ivory' series were good sellers, and deservedly so. These bikes were attractive in appearance and beautifully engineered. The range included 250cc, 350cc and 500cc machines capable of up to 85 mph and with fuel economy approaching 100 mpg. The author has seen a copy of a receipt for a 1934 500cc Calthorpe which changed hands in 1949 for the princely sum of £25. If only you could get a classic for that price today....

Sadly these later (more expensive) bikes were not made in great numbers and the company declined in the 1930s, as was the typical story in the financial conditions of that decade. Calthorpe were declared bankrupt in 1938 and a couple of subsequent revival attempts using Matchless and Villiers engines proved unsuccessful.

The J. A. Prestwich Engines

John Alfred Prestwich, born in Kensington, London, in 1874, was an extremely gifted engineer (as were several of his family members) who established his own company in 1895. Initially the firm produced scientific instruments and was highly involved in the fledgling film industry. Prestwich patented a movie projector using twin lenses in an attempt to solve the problem of flickering. Indeed, the company even undertook a limited film production role, filming such events as Queen Victoria's Diamond Jubilee procession in 1897. Prestwich continued to design and manufacture cinema equipment for the next 20 years even while expanding the company to build internal combustion engines.

The JAP engines covered a vast range. In addition to motorcycles, Prestwich made engines for chainsaws, rotavators, water pumps, milking machines, lawnmowers and even aircraft, but it was their motorcycle engines which ensured that the Prestwich name would be most widely known and remembered. Indeed, for a brief period (1904-08) JAP produced complete motorcycles, but the main focus was on supplying engines to other makers. Having moved to premises in Tottenham in 1911, the factory would remain in production until 1963.

The first JAP engine, a single-cylinder overhead-valve four-stroke, had an ingenious design which allowed a single pushrod to operate both the inlet and exhaust valve. This was available in both 2¼-hp and 3½-hp versions from 1903. Even the spark plugs were of Prestwich design, and in keeping with the firm's philosophy of supplying every available market, the plugs were made available separately for other non-JAP engines.

The range expanded rapidly, with the first overhead-valve V-twin appearing in 1906. This was to become the 'classic' JAP layout, although three-cylinder designs, specialist

The original JAP single-pushrod overhead-valve
motorcycle engine. (*Courtesy of Grace's Guide*)

engines such as a 1910 V8 aero engine and a patented desmodromic-valve system (in
1923) demonstrated that JAP continued to develop and innovate over many years.

Desmo systems, now associated in most people's minds with Ducati, use a second
cam to close the valves in place of a spring. In fact, a small spring is often used to assist
in sealing the valve fully, especially at low speeds and when the engine is cold, but the
use of a mechanical closing mechanism prevents the valve 'floating' at high revs – and
possibly even meeting the piston with disastrous results. In the early days the production
of reliable valve springs was a considerable metallurgical problem. In fact, BRM were
having major troubles with the springs in their Formula One car engines as late as 1960.
Graham Hill, who was driving for them at the time, reported in his autobiography
Life at the Limit, that he even took some springs to his own small tuning company,
Speedwell Conversions, to be re-treated, and that 'a few of them did last a race or two'.
Stirling Moss had difficulty adapting to the 'wrong way round' gate on the Mercedes
gearbox when he moved to them early in his Grand Prix career and has credited their
Desmo valve system with saving his engine on one or two occasions.

Speedway was to prove enormously important to the JAP business, but it took a
while for John Prestwich to be convinced of its potential. Sometime in 1928, engineer

Stan Greening (who later rose to become JAP's Chief Technical Advisor), having visited Stamford Bridge Speedway, was first to suggest that the fledgling sport could prove important. Opinions vary as to the precise beginnings of Speedway, but it had only appeared in Britain a year or so previously and Prestwich considered it to be a passing craze saying it would 'burst like a bubble' in six months or less. However, at the 1929 Olympia Motorcycle Show, the Stamford Bridge captain, Bill Bragg, visited the JAP stand and spoke to Vivian Prestwich, the eldest of John P's five sons and a racing enthusiast.

Douglas horizontally opposed twin engines were dominant in Speedway at that point, but Bragg was convinced that a development of the JAP single could be far superior. He suggested a radical approach: using the cylinder of a 500cc engine, minus about half the depth of its cooling fins since Speedway races are short (the four laps take little more than one minute to complete), and saving further weight by mounting the cylinder onto the crankcase of a much smaller 344cc racing engine and fitting the head from a road-going 350cc engine on the top. Vivian found Bragg's suggestions convincing and prevailed on his father to change his mind. As a result, Greening was given approval to develop a Speedway engine along the lines which Bragg had suggested.

As might be imagined, the engineering difficulties were considerable. A large amount of material had to be removed from the base flange of the cylinder, while additional

A 'skinny' 500cc JAP 4B single, installed in a successful, though venerable, sprint machine; a beautifully prepared 'Young Special' dating from 1936. Sprinting is essentially similar to drag racing except whereas drag races are run over a smooth quarter-mile strip, sprints are more 'flexible'.

metal had to be welded onto the undersize head. When the engine, designated the JAP 4B, was first tested at the Crystal Palace Speedway, Bragg's fellow riders were of the opinion that the rather 'skinny' looking motor would blow up in a shower of metal. It didn't do that, but it wasn't as powerful as the four-valve Rudge which had begun to replace the Douglas as the power unit of choice.

Happily for JAP, the famed rider and engineer Wal Phillips, whose uncle Bert LeVack worked for Prestwich, sometimes came to visit his uncle at the Prestwich factory. Phillips owned a Rudge Speedway bike and he agreed to work with Greening to strip it down and study it. Lessons were learned and problems solved (and apparently neighbours annoyed by late night testing!) but Greening was able to make changes to port sizes and angles, valve timing and other engine parameters. Soon after, Phillips rode the JAP engine to wins in its first two races and broke the track record into the bargain at Stamford Bridge. JAP now had an engine which developed 33 bhp and weighed only 53 lbs (about 24 kg) and when Wal won his Gold Star at Brooklands by lapping at 106.5 mph on a Grindlay-Peerless with the JAP Speedway engine installed, it lost any reputation for fragility which might have lingered in riders' minds.

It became necessary to tool up for mass production at the JAP factory in Tottenham as Speedway riders realised that their evening's pay depended on using JAP power. Soon the demand reached a point at which it became impractical to supply private buyers directly from the factory. An independent company, Victor Martin Ltd, was set up to be run by a former Prestwich employee who had been involved in the development of the engine. Martin manufactured the Rudge frame under licence and was therefore able to sell complete 500cc Speedway racing machines. Initially (in 1933) these sold for £87.

The JAP engine remained the top choice – indeed, the almost universal choice – among Speedway riders from its introduction in 1930 all the way through to the merger with Villiers in 1957, after which time the Jawa engine came to the fore. In the early years many modifications were made and the power was increased. The crankcase castings were replaced with stronger mounting lugs and increased internal stiffening. The connecting rod and cylinder barrel were lengthened slightly to reduce stress on the big end. The original cast iron rocker stands were changed for alloy ones and an additional cylinder head bolt was added to maintain reliability as the output increased to 40 bhp.

After the Second World War, a new cylinder head casting with more metal around the exhaust port enabled the engine to revert to its original four-stud layout, but remarkably few other specification changes were required since the engine was not being seriously challenged. The 4B found a second application in four-wheeled racing as its light weight and high compression made it ideal for the early 500cc Formula Three cars built by the likes of John Cooper. It was eventually superseded by the Norton engine.

The JAP company merged with Villiers Engineering in 1957 and engine manufacture was moved from Tottenham to Wolverhampton in 1962.

The Card Era

Alec Card, who died in 2010, was one of those young men who found it easier to afford a motorcycle than a car in the years following the Second World War. Unlike most, however, he managed to buy a Brough Superior SS80. The bike had a sidecar attached and he used this to make riding safer in the winter, but he rode solo in summer. He gained an affection for Broughs which lasted a lifetime.

Having gained qualifications as an engineer, he went on to build frames for Speedway machines; of course, JAP engines, already well known to him through the Brough connection, were highly successful in Speedway. Card progressed to working on engines and by the 1970s he had designed major replacement components for JAP machinery. He approached Norton (who owned the JAP factory at the time) and asked permission to use the JAP name on engines built using his own crankcases. When permission was not forthcoming, Card checked his facts and found that although Norton had bought JAP's premises and existing stocks, the actual name was still available.

Not only did he now buy the name, but he rapidly began to develop his own complete engine. The first prototype 'new old' JAP V-twin, built in the late 70s, is still running today in a Morgan three-wheeler and holds hill-climb records at various venues.

Joined by his son Dave, Card began to produce his JAP engines for customers in 1980, but remained true to the innovative ethos of the original company. These modern engines feature such high-tech components as ceramic cylinder liners and are available with fuel injection to meet modern emission regulations. In addition to complete new engines, the company now produce and sell a range of replacement parts for earlier JAP motors.

Along the way Alec also bought the rights to the Brough name. He sold this again when money was needed for the JAP business, but not before he had built himself a replica of the Bert LeVack record breaker of the 1920s. This bike features a modern JAP V-twin engine (obviously) and a hand-made springer fork (*see Glossary*), along with a modern replica frame and a three-speed Sturmey-Archer type gearbox. The company has recently announced the arrival of an all-new bobber-style† JAP motorcycle, powered by their V-twin and featuring a hard-tail frame and springer fork.

---

† Bobbers were early custom bikes featuring a cut-down, or 'bobbed', rear mudguard and differ from the more recent choppers in using a standard frame with conventional steering geometry and generally lacking heavy chrome work.

Chapter 2

Villiers, Sunbeam and the Marston Family

In 1898 John Marston was a cycle manufacturer with a problem. He believed in truly high standards of quality and finish, but was unable to obtain pedals for his machines which met these requirements. In 1898 he sent his son Charles to America to seek a solution.

This may seem excessive; how difficult can it be to make pedals? Marston's bicycles had, for almost a decade, incorporated his patented eccentric chain adjuster which used a moveable pedal crank and thus allowed a fixed rear axle. The need to adjust both sides of the axle equally, still a familiar problem for many motorcycle owners today, was eliminated. By 1898 the cranks were fitted with a beautiful epicyclic (*see Glossary*) two-speed gear and the chain was fully enclosed in an oil bath. The machines were selling well and large numbers of accurately engineered components were urgently needed.

Charles Marston appears to have found what he wanted when he visited the firm of Francis Pratt and Amos Whitney, whose company later provided finance and a name to Frederick Rentshler's fledgling Pratt and Whitney Aircraft Company. By the time of Marston's visit, Pratt and Whitney's dedication to accurate measurement in engineering had already generated several machine tool patents. It is quite likely that the Americans supplied Marston with the tooling he needed to make his bicycle pedals, but he was certainly impressed by the assembly line production techniques he discovered in America.

There was no room for this in the existing 'courtyard' style works in which the Marstons built their 'Sunbeam' bicycles, and so premises were bought in Villiers Street, Wolverhampton. This new factory was registered as the Villiers Cycle Component Company and Charles Marston became its Managing Director.

Villiers

Although only eight men were employed here initially, the Villiers factory, with its modern equipment and methods, was able to produce far more parts than Sunbeam needed, and the excess was sold to other cycle makers. Villiers became a significant manufacturer in its own right, and by 1902 the workforce had more than quadrupled. Charles Marston appointed Frank Farrer, who was to become a major force in the company, as agent to sell the pedals.

At some point, John Marston sold the Villiers factory to his son and in 1902 Villiers patented the bicycle freewheel. These were such an instant success that every other manufacturer had to fit them to its bicycles in order to sell them; within two years Villiers had stopped producing pedals altogether! The freewheel remained a major Villiers product; in the mid-1940s they were making 80,000 each week for sale worldwide.

In the years immediately before the First World War, thoughts turned to the production of petrol engines. The first Villiers motorcycle engine was an unusual 'inlet-over-exhaust' (IOE) 350cc four-stroke, introduced in 1912 (*see Glossary*). This had a built-in two-speed gearbox and clutch, but cycle makers considered it too complicated and as a result it did not sell well.

It was Frank Farrer who championed the two-stroke, in the face of considerable opposition. Many experts felt that two-strokes had already been tried and found to be a dead end. But Farrer was persistent and Marston eventually wrote an instruction 'to oblige Mr Farrer, make him a two-stroke engine!'

This engine was an extremely simple 269cc motor with only three moving parts – the cast iron piston, the con-rod and the crankshaft – and simple phosphor-bronze bearings for the crankshaft and small end. Only the big end benefitted from a roller bearing. When Farrer tested the prototype he reported to Marston that they could sell thousands of them. This turned out to be incorrect, as they actually sold about 2½ million in numerous versions over a total production life of several decades.

The engine was lubricated using a hand-operated pump which fed oil through a drilled bolt into the crankcase, where oilways led it to the bearings. Surplus oil splashing onto the cylinder walls was carried up to the combustion chamber with the incoming charge of petrol/air mixture.

Relatively few engines were made during the First World War as the factory focused on producing munitions, but one outcome for Villiers was the development of a combined flywheel/magneto unit – since most magnetos had previously been imported from Germany. This new unit was incorporated into virtually all subsequent Villiers engines.

The first batch, designated the Mark 1 in spite of the earlier four-stroke, used an aluminium exhaust, but this was replaced with steel on the Mark 2 from 1916 onwards. In 1920 the Mark 3 featured a new flywheel centre to allow the engine to be used with either a sprocket (on a motorcycle) or a pulley (in stationary applications). Electric lighting was provided for on the Mark 4 and from 1922 the 269cc engine was replaced by a range of three (147cc, 247cc and 342cc) very similar engines. The first Villiers twin appeared in 1927. This had a capacity of 344cc and was built in a unit with clutch and three-speed gearbox. It also had automatic lubrication – no need to pump the oil!

As with JAP engines, the Villiers two-strokes were used in a full range of applications, although their main market was the burgeoning motorcycle industry, with advertising emphasising the lightness and affordability of Villiers-powered machines. A 1928 advert showed a woman riding a Villiers-engined machine and a man apparently carrying one under his arm, together with the statement, 'Twenty famous British makers fit Villiers engines to sturdy economical motor cycles.' It is interesting that the advert was for 'Villiers Two-Strokes'. Seemingly they felt that the engine defined the bike, almost regardless of the cycle maker.

This philosophy was perhaps taken to its logical conclusion with the 98cc Villiers Midget and the Junior 'autocycle' engine. Villiers encouraged various manufacturers to design machines around these engines and the Junior was taken up by Excelsior (the British one; there were entirely separate companies using this name in America and in Germany), James, Rudge, Coventry-Eagle, Francis-Barnett, Three Spires, Sun and a number of others. The name 'autocycle' actually dates back to the beginning of motorcycling, when it was simply a synonym for 'motorcycle', and it survives in this form in the name of the Auto Cycle Union – the ACU – the governing body of British Motorcycle sport. However, in the years between the wars it referred to bicycles with auxiliary engines and to the type of machine now called a moped.

Autocycles were considered useful to people in essential services like Air Raid Wardens and nurses; production was allowed to continue throughout the War. As a result, motorcycles were introduced to many people who might not otherwise have considered owning one. It is claimed that as many as 100,000 may have been sold – all with the reliable little Villiers Junior engine fitted.

Advert for a motorized bicycle powered by the Villiers Junior engine. (*Courtesy of Grace's Guide*)

Over the subsequent years, Villiers manufactured a large range of small two-stroke engines for both motorcycle and stationary applications, but they expanded the range into the larger and more powerful end of the market with the JAP merger in 1957. Now at last they were able to claim 'jointly, the two companies produce a vast range of two-stroke and four-stroke petrol engines and four-stroke diesel engines from $^1/3^{rd}$ to 16 bhp.' In 1965 the company was taken over by Manganese Bronze Holdings and, together with AMC, eventually became part of Norton-Villiers-Triumph. NVT went into receivership in 1974.

Sunbeam

We have already met John Marston and seen how his pursuit of high quality pedals led to the establishment of one of the great engine manufacturers Villiers, but it should not be forgotten that as a bicycle maker he had already founded the Sunbeam marque.

The quality of these bicycles was remarkable. It sprang in large part from John Marston's character – he was a perfectionist – but also from his original trade as a 'Japanner'. Japan black is a lacquer which can be applied directly to metal surfaces and then baked at around 200°C to produce a hard, glossy black finish which is highly durable. In the Victorian era, Japanning was popular as a decorative and hardwearing finish for both pottery and metal items and few homes would not possess some Japanned objects. As a result a thriving Japanning industry grew up in the Wolverhampton area and it was here that John Marston served his apprenticeship at the Jeddo works of Edward Perry, himself a significant figure and later twice Mayor of Wolverhampton.

Japanning was used as a finish in the early car industry, for example forming the basis of Henry Ford's famous black Model T.

When Marston later bought the Jeddo works on Perry's death and began to build his bicycles, he naturally used this excellent quality of black finish. It is said (truthfully or otherwise) that it was Marston's wife Ellen who named them 'Sunbeam' because of the way the light reflected off the high gloss surfaces. Even the works were renamed 'Sunbeamland'.

Marston's machines were not just good to look at. Sunbeam pioneered a range of mechanical improvements and gained a reputation which encouraged leading figures of the day to ride them. Sir Edward Elgar bought two and took them back to the factory regularly to have them maintained in perfect condition.

This was Sunbeam's advertised promise to its customers:

Most cycle makers are now struggling to produce the <u>Cheapest</u> Bicycle. Yet a rider's life depends, not upon the cheapness of his bicycle, but upon its <u>soundness</u>. No "competitive price" bicycles are made at Sunbeamland. Cyclists who buy these machines need, therefore, be under no apprehension of becoming victims to the "war of prices".

These pages: A pair of immaculately prepared Sunbeams, one of which is the TT-winning Model 90TT, showing off John Marston's superb 'Japanned' black finish and the patented 'Little Oil Bath' chain case.

After an early flirtation with powered cycles in which a man was killed (though no-one seems to have recorded his name), Marston avoided them for many years and diversified into car-making instead. However, a slump in car sales forced him into building motorcycles from 1912 onwards, at the age of 76, and following his life-long tradition, he produced high quality machines, mostly single cylinder, which were sold as 'The Gentleman's Machine'.

By the time Marston entered the motorcycle market the belt drive era had essentially passed and from the start his machines were fitted with a version of the same 'little oil bath' chain drive already developed for Sunbeam bicycles. The first of Marston's gentlemen's motorcycles used the 349cc inlet-over-exhaust single-cylinder engine which was made at the Villiers Street works. This 1912 engine was rated at 2¾ hp and Harry Stevens of AJS motorcycles was commissioned by Marston to design it. A major appointment was now made at Sunbeam: John Greenwood, who had formerly been with JAP, was taken on to design a motorcycle around the Stevens engine. Greenwood went on to design almost all subsequent Sunbeam engines. The original Stevens 350cc model was discontinued in 1915 and this engine size remained absent from the range until 1923 when the Models 1 and 2 revived it using a narrower cylinder bore and correspondingly longer stroke in accordance with the contemporary tax laws.† This would be the last side-valve 350cc engine from Sunbeam; all subsequent models in the class used overhead-valve engines.

It was in 1913 that Greenwood's first Sunbeam engine appeared. Rated at 3½ hp, this was a 499cc motor with a bore and stroke of 85 x 88 mm. This bike laid the foundations for Sunbeam's success in the early years of the Isle of Man TT, achieving a second place finish in the 1914 Senior Race and winning the Manufacturer's Award.

Marston added a larger model powered by a 6-hp JAP V-twin of 770cc capacity and capable of pulling a sidecar. This was produced until difficulties with the supply of JAP engines forced a change to units made by AKD and the Swiss firm MAG in 1915/16. The MAG was a slightly bigger 8-hp design and possibly gave the machine even more capability as a sidecar puller.

Sunbeam were able to revert to JAP power before the end of the First World War, but this time they chose the 996cc engine in order to further enhance the bike's suitability for sidecar work. This version of the V-twin was produced until 1923. There was also a smaller 5-hp V-twin, which was made during the War as a solo machine for the Russian Army, but this did not enter civilian production.

---

† The description of engines by horsepower ratings depends on a formula developed by the RAC. This assigns an 'indicated' horse power to each engine, based on the diameter of its cylinders and the number of cylinders. It makes three basic assumptions relating to the mean pressure in the cylinder during a power stroke, the mean speed of a piston at the engine's highest revs and the mechanical efficiency of the engine. As all three of the assumed values were soon exceeded due to engineering advances it follows that actual brake horse power soon exceeded 'indicated power', but the formula survived because it had been used as a basis for vehicle taxation – and this continued long after the formula became effectively obsolete. Of course, it also follows that long-stroke engines with narrow bores were cheaper to tax and so the formula exerted an influence on engine design for many years.

It was the 3½-hp 'Standard' machine, also called the Model 3, which was introduced in 1915, which became something of a general purpose workhorse during the First World War. The Model 3, again with an engine designed by John Greenwood, remained in production until 1926 and by 1920 these side valve machines were winning on the Isle of Man. As the decade progressed further, development under riders such as George Dance and Graham Walker made Sunbeam one of the most successful marques; their bikes were certainly a match for anything else then racing. They won events as diverse as the Ulster Grand Prix, the Bol D'Or, the Italian Grand Prix and the Southport Rough Riders Trial, many of these on several occasions, and set numerous standing-start and flying-start speed records.

The Longstroke Model 6 was given a successful 'test run' by Alexander Bennett in winning the 1921 French Grand Prix at Strasbourg, and went into production the following year. The bike, whose 77 x 105.5-mm 492cc engine was the fastest single-cylinder side-valve design of its day, became the last side-valve-engined machine to win the Senior TT when Bennett rode it to victory in 1922. It was to remain a fixture in the Sunbeam catalogue for the next 17 years. The original flat tank was changed to a saddle type along with other stylistic changes before ICI bought out Sunbeam in 1929. At this point it gained the model name 'Lion' and the ICI Lion logo on its tank. The Longstroke Lion continued in manufacture even after the AMC takeover of 1937.

The Model 4 was short-lived, remaining on sale for only a little over two years, spanning the period 1924-26. This was a 600cc bike using the cycle parts of the Standard model and a 596cc engine developed for the 1922 Model 7. The Model 7 itself retained the Standard model's 85-mm bore, but extended the stroke to match the 105.5 mm of the Longstroke. This gave a capacity of 596cc and it replaced the JAP V-twin as the company's sidecar-pulling machine. The Model 7 gained fame (or notoriety?) for retaining a flat tank long after all other makers had moved on to saddle tanks. The flat tank Model 7 actually was retained well into the 1930s, by which time it must have looked very old fashioned. It was finally replaced by the saddle tanked Model 7A, which was also known as the 600cc Lion. This was produced until 1940, by which time the basic design was approaching 20 years old.

John Greenwood's original 'square stroke' engine (85 x 88 mm) had gained a significant following among riders with its sporty performance; the Model 5 Light Solo of 1923 was intended also to appeal to these riders. It featured the light frame of the Longstroke combined with the Standard's 499cc TT-winning engine and was produced until 1926.

Following the AMC takeover in September 1937, Sunbeam motorcycles were produced for a few years in London from Wolverhampton-made parts. AMC also built their own bikes based on previous Sunbeam designs until the Second World War put a stop to civilian production. The Sunbeam name and trademarks were sold to BSA in 1943 and many enthusiasts regard this as the end of the true Marston/Sunbeam line.

Nevertheless, the immediate postwar years saw BSA/Sunbeam announce a new 487cc model based on an in-line twin engine with an integral four-speed gearbox. This bike, to be known as the S7, appeared to boast virtually everything that the pre-war motorcycling public had been asking for – shaft drive, overhead cams, a plunger-type sprung rear end – in fact, in addition to such things, a total of thirty newly patented features were on show.

Yet somehow the new bike seemed a bit too much like a car. Certainly the design seemed to have originated on the drawing board of a car designer, and the public hesitated to rush out and buy it. The S7 was heavy and, at 24 bhp, underpowered. As a result it had a top speed of only just over 70 mph. A sports version was promised, but it fell foul of one of the patented new S7 features. Owing to the low position of the gearbox output shaft, the drive to the rear wheel was by an underslung worm gear. Worms have their place in engineering of course (model trains and some stairlifts spring to mind!), but they normally have low ratios and do not lend themselves well to high-speed applications. In an attempt to overcome this limitation, the Sunbeam designers had introduced a strong skew to the teeth of the roller and this led to increased friction. Even in the kind of touring use for which the S7 was suited, this final drive unit ran hot and when the power was increased it wore at an unacceptable rate. Instead of switching to a more conventional drive, Sunbeam decided that the sports project was impractical and it was simply abandoned.

In its original form, the S7 engine had been bolted directly to the frame and extreme vibration had afflicted the production models. It has been suggested that this was not picked up in development testing simply because the development bikes were manufactured to closer tolerances. To overcome the problem, rubber mountings were

The Sunbeam S8, showing the flexible section of exhaust pipe which was added to permit the engine to move on its rubber mountings. The main difference between the S8 and the earlier S7 is the use of conventional BSA forks and a standard size tyre to replace the 'fat' tyre used on the S7.

added at an early stage, but this meant that the engine could move relative to the frame and so a short flexible section had to be added to the exhaust. This 'workaround' measure was retained throughout the life of the S7/8 models.

The S8 model was introduced in 1949. This weighed significantly less than the S7 as the front forks had been replaced with those from the BSA A10 (Sunbeam machines were by this time being made in the BSA works at Redditch). The S7's telescopic forks had been of an unusual layout. The hydraulic damping mechanisms were inside the fork legs in the conventional way but the springs were placed in a separate housing above the front wheel. As an additional encouragement to potential buyers, the S8 was also £30 cheaper than the S7 – an appreciable amount in 1949. But in spite of such moves, the S8 never really sold in the numbers which would have generated enthusiasm at BSA, and although production continued until 1956, there was to be no S9.

The Colliers, already owners of Matchless, added AJS to their portfolio in 1931 and bought Sunbeam in 1937. The company was renamed Amalgamated Motorcycles Limited and this was further modified to Associated Motorcycles (AMC) the following year. Interestingly, and presumably as an attempt to maintain a distinction between the two marques, the Japanned black and gold finish which had been the hallmark of Sunbeam machines since James Marston's day continued to be used on AJS machines, but was not transferred to Matchless models. The photograph shows a 500cc Matchless G50 in its typical red paintwork. Compare this machine with the 350cc AJS 7R seen on pages 122/3.

The 500cc Matchless G50 is virtually identical to the AJS 7R in all but colour.

Chapter 3

The Motorcycle as a Racing Machine

No story of this kind can be complete without consideration of the importance of racing, both for development and as advertising. No race has been as influential throughout virtually the entire story of motorcycling as the Isle of Man Tourist Trophy – 'the TT', along with its amateur partner, the Manx Grand Prix. From the earliest beginnings of the TT in 1905, machines which won the TT were successful machines, and factories which won the TT sold motorbikes. The races no longer have World Championship status due to the severity and danger of the Mountain Course, but racers still queue for entries – there were over sixty competitors in the Newcomers race at the 2012 MGP for example. Indeed, no less a person than Murray Walker (whose father Graham himself won fifteen silver replicas in the event) has described the TT as the greatest motorsport event of any kind in the world. Any motorcyclist referring simply to 'the island' will expect to be understood, and it follows that many TT and MGP winners can be found in these pages.

There are a very large number of prizes to be won by those who dare to race on the Isle of Man Mountain Course. Many people and organisations have endowed awards. There are prizes for newcomers, local riders, older riders and more. A finisher's medal is an honour in itself and many competitors are satisfied to achieve one. Starting a Manx Grand Prix race entitles the rider to life membership of the Manx Grand Prix Riders Association.

At the 'sharp end' of the scale is the TT Senior Trophy, a truly magnificent colossus in silver. First awarded to Charlie Collier in 1907, the trophy carries the name of Joseph the Marquis de Mouzilly St Mars, who originally suggested the establishment of the race and donated the Italian-designed 108-cm-tall trophy. It was actually 20 cm shorter in 1907, but has had to be extended to accommodate more shields for the winners' names. Every Senior winner is there and a further extension will soon be needed!

The trophy is modelled on the Montague Trophy, which was awarded to the winner of the Tourist Trophy for cars, a race which predated the motorcycle event by a few years. The plinth is surmounted by a silver model representing Mercury standing on a winged wheel and the entire trophy weighs almost 24 kg. Nowadays the trophy is insured for £1.5 million and is kept permanently on the Isle of Man. This was not

Above: Action at the TT. Cameron Donald leads his team-mate Bruce Anstey off the mountain.

Right: Manxman Dan Kneen displays his silver replica awarded for a fifth place finish in the 2010 Supersport TT. At the time of writing Dan is the only rider ever to have won three Manx Grand Prix races in the same year.

always the case; back in the 1930s, for example, the winner was allowed to keep the trophy for a year, which meant that following a German win for Georg Meier in 1939 the trophy left the island for the duration of the Second World War. Its whereabouts were unknown for a time and it was eventually discovered on display in a Viennese shop. The winning factory BMW fared worse, however, spending the war buried in a field!

Silver replicas of the trophy are awarded to riders who finish within 105 per cent of the winner's time and bronze replicas go to those finishing within 110 per cent.

The TT has been run for more than 100 years, and for a full century the same course has been used. True, it has been hugely upgraded over the years – what road hasn't? – but it follows the same 37¾-mile route through towns and villages, along country lanes and over 'the mountain'. Snaefell stands 2,034 feet (621 metres) above sea level and the course passes close by the summit. Only one small 400-yard section of the course at the very end of the lap is no longer used for everyday traffic, and at the time of writing (2012) the lap record stands to John McGuiness at 17 minutes 12.3 seconds

The view over Ramsey from the marshalling post at the Guthrie monument. Can there be a more beautiful race circuit anywhere?

– an *average* speed of just over 131 mph. Those who compete are among the bravest sportsmen and women in the world, and any bike which completes a six-lap race has been tested to an extreme degree.

With an eye to the future, there is now a race for electric machines at the TT, and the 100-mph lap has already been achieved in this event.

Geoff Duke

Geoffrey Ernest Duke OBE was virtually synonymous with motorcycle racing in the public mind in the 1950s. He won a total of six world championships and five TTs and his name was spoken in almost hushed tones on the Isle of Man where he was often referred to simply as 'The Duke'. Indeed, it is still so among many of the older Manx residents and a section of three sharp bends between Brandywell and Windy Corner on the TT Course are now known collectively as 'Duke's'.

His victories in both the Clubman's Senior TT and the Senior Manx Grand Prix in 1949 brought him to prominence and he was snapped up by the Norton works team for 1950. This was only the second year of the 500cc World Championship and Duke almost rewarded Norton by winning it. His year started well with new lap and race records on his way to winning the Senior TT, and also included wins at the Ulster Grand Prix and the Nations GP which was held at Monza, but mechanical failures caused him to miss out on points at the Belgian GP and the Dutch TT. In spite of this, he only lost by a single point to the eventual champion, the Italian Umberto Masetti.

Duke was able to put this disappointment behind him in 1951 though, winning both the 350cc and 500cc World Championships with a total of seven wins across the two classes. Injuries sustained in a non-championship race put paid to his hopes of back to back 500cc wins in 1952, but he had enough points to hold on to his 350cc title.

For 1953 The Duke provoked controversy, in Britain at least, by leaving Norton and signing for the Italian manufacturer, Gilera. It was certainly a successful decision, however, as he won three consecutive premier class championships in 1953, 1954 and 1955. There might well have been a fourth, but in 1956 he was banned from the first two Grand Prix as a reprisal for his support of a riders' strike over better pay for privateers. John Surtees won on the MV in the Duke's absence, and although Duke won the Italian GP and Surtees suffered a broken arm late in the year, Surtees' points lead was sufficient to take the overall prize.

Duke's hopes for 1957 were again dashed by injury, as he was forced to miss four of the six rounds – but he still managed to finish fourth in the table. Gilera withdrew from racing in 1958, leaving Duke to sign for BMW for the 500cc Championship and return to Norton for a 350cc ride, but neither of these machines was a match for the MV Agusta which was now dominant. Duke did not stay with BMW but moved to Norton for the 500cc class mid-season and was the top non-MV finisher in both championships. He stayed with the British company for 1959, and enduring another mediocre season chasing the MVs, he felt he had nothing left to prove and retired from racing at the end of the year.

During the 1955 TT, Duke was announced to have achieved the first ever 100-mph lap of the Mountain Course, only to have this declared an error shortly afterwards. The corrected speed was then stated to have been only 99.97 mph and the first 'ton-up' lap eventually went to Bob McIntyre, also on a Gilera, in 1957. The difference is less than 0.5 of a second and some have cried 'foul', arguing that the timing equipment available in 1955 was not accurate enough to make this call reliably. That claim is probably correct, but this author would accept that race officials have no option but to accept the start and finish times recorded by the timekeepers, and to make their calculations on that basis. It follows that any error discovered in the calculations themselves would have to be corrected. It was clearly tough for Duke and his supporters though.

Duke felt that the two-piece leathers worn by all riders previously were not as effective as they could be and enlisted the help of his tailor to make him a one-piece suit. This had the clear advantage that it could not separate at the waist in an accident and he was therefore the first rider to wear what is now considered an essential piece of safety equipment in motorcycle racing.

In addition to his motorcycling successes, Geoff Duke raced on four wheels in the Sebring 12-hour race of 1953, driving an Aston Martin DB3 in partnership with Peter Collins. They failed to finish after Duke crashed.

He was named Sportsman of the Year in 1951, awarded the RAC Segrave Trophy, and in recognition of his services to motorcycling, was awarded the Order of the British Empire in 1953. The FIM named him a 'Grand Prix Legend' in 2002.

Brooklands

Brooklands was built at the personal expense of wealthy landowner Hugh Lock King near Weybridge in Surrey in 1907. He may have intended it purely as a motor racing circuit, but it rapidly came to be a centre of excellence for the emerging technologies of the age. Cars, motorcycles and aircraft all found a home at Brooklands, with factories

A surviving section of the Brooklands banking as it appeared in 2008. (*Courtesy of Ron Coombs*)

and sheds of every size occupied by adventurous young men willing to take risks and develop new ideas. Tommy Sopwith built his Camels at Brooklands.

Motor racing at Brooklands continued until the outbreak of the Second World War, and British Aerospace maintained manufacturing facilities there until 1987.

The motor racing circuit itself, the first purpose-built race venue in the world, was designed for Lock King by Colonel H. C. L. Holden of the Royal Artillery and had a lap length of 2¾ miles plus a 'finishing straight' adding an extra ½ mile. At this time British roads were covered by a blanket 20-mph speed limit and this was obviously more than slightly restrictive to those with a craving for high-speed thrills. It was also feared by many that the British car and motorcycle industries would be stifled by the lack of opportunity for high-speed testing; the French, in particular, were seen to be making great strides. Just a glance at the track's layout will show the importance attached to sustained speed. Two high bankings (the Home, or Members' banking and the Byfleet banking) allowed any driver (who dared) to maintain full throttle for virtually the entire lap. Large sections of these bankings remain to this day and they are impressive to say the least. A dotted black line, known as the 50-foot line, ran along the centre of the road, and it was intended that a car following this line would follow the curve without any input from the steering wheel – providing it was going fast enough. It was not possible to surface the 100-foot-wide thirty-foot-high bankings with tarmac, and so large concrete slabs were used. These settled unevenly over time and many contemporary photographs show cars travelling at high speed with all four wheels off the ground due to the bumps!

Motorcycle racing began at Brooklands in 1908 and the British Motor Cycle Racing Club was formed in 1909. The club's full name was appropriate and descriptive of course, but a bit of a mouthful to use in conversation, so it was commonly abbreviated to 'The Bemsee' by its members. Sidecar racers joined the solos in 1912, although it is known that many manufacturers were unhappy to see their homely products 'abused' in this way. Despite any such objections there was a regular 200-mile race for these machines which remained a popular fixture on the Brooklands calendar for several years.

It is surely possible that the Americans took some inspiration from Holden's track when they opened the Indianapolis Motor Speedway only two years after the first race at Weybridge. Their solution to the surfacing problem was to use a brick surface and Indianapolis has retained its 'Brickyard' nickname. There is still one yard of bricks across the start/finish line.

John Surtees

Only one man has ever won both the 500cc World Motorcycle Championship and the Formula One title as well. That man is John Surtees OBE.

Surtees' father was a three-time British sidecar champion and motorcycle dealer from South London, and so John grew up among bikes and bikers. His first taste of racing (and winning) actually came when he rode the sidecar of his father's Vincent although, as John was under age, they were promptly disqualified.

He entered his first solo grass-track race at the age of 15 and the following year began work as an apprentice at the Vincent works. He bought himself a car while working for Vincent, a Jowett Jupiter, made in Bradford by the same company which had manufactured the earliest Scott motorcycles under contract to Alfred Scott.

At the age of 17, in 1951, Surtees made his first big impression as a rider by putting Geoff Duke's works Norton under heavy pressure in a race at Thruxton, an extremely fast race circuit near Andover in Hampshire. He would have to wait until 1955 to actually beat world champion Duke, but he did it twice that year, at Silverstone and Brands Hatch, and he was by then a works rider in his own right, Norton chief Joe Craig presumably having kept an eye on the fast Londoner.

Sadly, Norton were in financial decline by this time and their future in racing was in doubt, but Surtees received an offer from MV Agusta which he accepted.

By the end of 1956 Surtees was the 500cc World Champion, admittedly having been helped along the way by the FIM decision to impose a six-month ban on Duke following his support of a riders' strike. Duke was now riding for Gilera and in 1957 the MV was no match for the other Italian bike, so Surtees had to settle for third place in the championship behind the Gileras of Libero Liberati and Bob McIntyre.

However, this was to be the last time an MV was 'no match' for another marque for a very long time. Both Gilera and Moto Guzzi pulled out of racing at the end of the '57 season and Surtees won three consecutive titles in 1958, 1959 and 1960, winning thirty-two out of the thirty-nine races and along the way becoming the first man to win the Senior TT three times in succession.

Astonishingly, after the disappointing 1957 season, the dominance of MV was so great that no other manufacturer won the 500cc World Championship until 1974. After Surtees' three wins, Rhodesian Gary Hocking won in 1961. The next four years belonged to Mike Hailwood, and then Giacomo Agostini made the championship his own for seven years before handing over to Phil Read for 1973 and 1974. Truly astonishing.

Why did Surtees not continue his winning run after 1960? He moved to four-wheel racing, making his Formula One debut at the 1960 Monaco Grand Prix. He finished second in his second Grand Prix, the 1960 British race, and achieved pole position in his third, in Portugal. Note that this was in his final championship year as a motorcyclist! And he was still only 26 years old.

He moved to Ferrari in 1963 and won the Formula One World Championship in 1964. In September 1965, Surtees had a life-threatening accident in a Lola T70 at Mosport in Canada, but recovered fully and won the inaugural Can-Am series, competing against the likes of Bruce McLaren and Chris Amon in their McLarens, which would later dominate the series.

Surtees' deteriorating relationship with Ferrari team manager Eugenio Dragoni has been documented elsewhere, but it culminated in a move to Honda for 1967 and probably cost him a second drivers' championship. There was a win in the Italian Grand Prix at Monza and fourth place in the championship, and Surtees was instrumental in assisting Honda to become a serious force in Formula One.

For the 1968 French Grand Prix they produced the air-cooled, magnesium-bodied RA302, but Surtees declined to drive it in the race as he felt it needed further development. His replacement, Joe Schlesser, died in a massive fire after losing control on the second lap in torrential rain, and shortly afterwards Honda withdrew from Grand Prix racing.

Surtees later formed his own team and built his own Formula One car and Formula Two and Formula 5000 cars. He retired from competitive driving in 1972, the same year in which another ex-motorcycle champion, Mike Hailwood, won the European Formula Two Championship in one of his cars.

In 1996, Surtees was inducted into the International Motorsports Hall of Fame and in 2003 the FIM named him as a 'Grand Prix Legend'. Already an MBE, he was appointed an OBE in the 2008 Birthday Honours.

Surtees' son Henry followed him into motorsport, competing successfully in karting for several seasons before moving up to the FIA Formula Two Championship. He was tragically killed in an accident at Brands Hatch in 2009.

Pendine Sands

Pendine Sands is a 7-mile stretch of smooth beach on Carmarthen Bay in South Wales, and was the scene of speed trials and races in the 1920s. The use of the Sands dates back to the time when the 20-mph limit was still in force and in order to even watch cars or motorcycles travelling fast in these early years of the twentieth century you needed to be able to afford the time and expense of a trip to the Isle of Man, or brave what many perceived as the 'upper class' atmosphere of fashionable Brooklands, known at the time as 'The Ascot of Motorsport'. Pendine provided an accessible alternative venue and was greeted with widespread enthusiasm. It attracted the top factory teams and the most famous riders, including such stars as Bert LeVack, George Dance and Freddie Dixon. It was reported that as many as 40,000 people came on foot, bicycle, train and charabanc to see races on the 2½-mile circuit which was laid out on the sands. Many camped out among the dunes and when the first 100-mile 'Welsh TT' was held in 1922, the *Motor Cycle* claimed that 'motorcycle racing is the finest of all sports'. Who could even think to accuse them of bias? Less open to such a suggestion is their correspondent's view that Pendine was 'The finest natural speedway imaginable'. After all, the surface was straighter and smoother than most main roads at the time.

Oddly, the event's name was changed in 1928, dropping the 'TT' tag. From then on it was called simply the 'Welsh Hundred' for reasons which seem to have been lost in the mists of time. However, another mystery, the disappearance of the trophy, was finally solved in 2001, due to the efforts of Welsh enthusiast Lynn Hughes.

The whereabouts of the Welsh TT Trophy, topped by a splendid bronze figure of a dragon, were unknown for more than 70 years. Theories (or guesses) abounded. Had it been melted in a fire? Or perhaps carried away by Welsh flood water? Maybe a rich man's servant had made off with it? Hughes set out to discover the truth, using his network of contacts in Vintage motorcycle circles, writing letters to the press, even

John Parry-Thomas at speed in *Babs*, Pendine, 1926.

getting a friend to check for clues on a graveyard memorial. All to no avail it seemed, except for one tantalising letter whose writer claimed to have seen the trophy in a garage belonging to C. P. 'Clarry' Wood, who won it twice in the '20s. If this were true, it suggested that the missing prize might at least have survived, but it appeared to be a dead end. No further progress was made until a book Hughes had written was reviewed in the *Telegraph*. A reader, Derek Wood, the son of Clarry Wood, phoned in. 'Was someone looking for the TT Trophy?' he asked. The Welsh TT Trophy was intact and safe and has since been displayed back at Pendine.

In the 1920s the Sands were used for Land Speed Record attempts. Malcolm Campbell and Henry Segrave ran there and the legendary 27-litre *Babs* car, in which John Parry-Thomas set a record speed of 171 mph in 1926, remained buried in the sand for several decades after his fatal crash in 1927. Dug out in the 1960s and restored to running condition, the car is now displayed at Brooklands for half the year and in the Pendine Museum of Speed for the remainder. No further LSR attempts were made at Pendine after Parry-Thomas' death until 2000, when Don Wales, the grandson of Malcolm Campbell (and nephew of Donald) set a United Kingdom record speed for electric vehicles. He achieved a speed of 137 mph in Bluebird Electric 2.

In 1933 Amy Johnson and her husband took off from Pendine to fly non-stop to New York. They made the flight successfully but crashed on landing and were both seriously injured.

Herbert 'Bert' LeVack

There is a long engineering history among Scots. Despite his apparently French surname, Bert LeVack was a Scot, though born in London in 1887. His grandfather had been a steam locomotive engineer and had moved to England from Caithness and so perhaps young Herbert was really just following a family tradition, but he was certainly a highly gifted motorcycle engineer and also a talented rider. This is not such a rare combination, but it is an enormously valuable one when development work is to be done.

His achievements in tuning motorcycles, winning races and setting speed records were to earn him the nickname 'The Wizard of Brooklands' in the 1920s, and he worked or rode at various times for JAP, Motosacoche, Indian, New Imperial, Brough Superior and New Hudson, though his first job was with a car maker, Legros and Knowles of Willesden.

After further work with Daimler, Napier and even the London General Omnibus Company, and some early experience of bicycle racing, LeVack discovered Brooklands. In or around 1909 he entered, and won, a hill-climb on a Triumph. In 1912 he competed in the London to Edinburgh run and he rode in the 1914 TT on a Motosacoche. He also survived an incident in which he almost succeeded in blowing himself up by looking in a petrol tank with a lighted match in the dark.

By the start of the First World War, LeVack had become an official JAP test rider, but when war intervened he and John Wallace, another tester, went to work on the design and manufacture of aero engines at the Scottish firm of Arrol-Johnston.

The 'test hill' was an important feature of Brooklands in these early days. Being able to get up a steep hill was a genuine test of a vehicle, whether two- or four-wheeled. Along with LeVack, Freddie Barnes of Zenith motorcycles was another important character who cut his racing teeth there, and the hill continued to host events until the First World War. After this it became gradually less relevant as developments in engines and gearboxes had removed the fundamental challenge. The final motorcycle record was set in 1936 when Francis Beart took his 500cc Grindlay-Peerless to the top in 6.99 seconds – a far cry from the first record set by Barnes at 18.63 seconds (an average speed of 12.89 mph).

After the war, LeVack ran a garage business for a while, but his interest in racing and the time he dedicated to tuning his Edmund machine meant that the business did not get the attention it needed. He was pleased to accept a job offer, on only a moderate salary, from his friend Wallace, who had also started his own business, Duzmo Motorcycles.

Wallace was a talented designer, but did not have the riding talent to go with it, and therefore the addition of Bert's skills played a large part in making Duzmo's name. They prospered together for a time, but it was probably inevitable that LeVack would receive an offer which he could not refuse, and which Wallace could not match.

The offer came towards the end of 1920 from the American Hendee Manufacturing Company, maker of Indian motorcycles in Springfield, Massachusetts. Hendee had a depot in London and it was here that LeVack worked on the new 8-valve Indian V-twin engine, known, to him at least, as the 'Camel'. In 1921 he won the prestigious Brooklands 500-mile race on an Indian Powerplus.

Following this, he seems to have felt patriotic as he returned to his previous employer, John A. Prestwich, as a designer with the avowed intention of helping JAP design and produce a 'Yank Buster'. The resulting 986cc overhead-valve V-twin, known as the 'Super Big Twin', found success in racing and record setting and was a natural power unit for the newly introduced Brough Superior. Indian dropped out of competition, though this was not necessarily cause and effect.

LeVack was a great believer in using alcohol-based fuels in racing engines, and had actually managed to obtain supplies from a London distillery. He had his own workshop in JAP's Tottenham factory, where along with other aspects of his work, he gained a reputation for his ability to blend 'special' fuels for the works engines.

Although he only stayed with JAP four years, LeVack's star status was such that he appeared in much of their advertising astride a Brough Superior; this time fitted with a 976cc V-twin.

Herbert LeVack was killed testing a Motosacoche in the Alps in 1931.

The Bol D'Or

The Bol D'Or is effectively motorcycle racing's equivalent of the Le Mans 24-hour race, with teams of three riders sharing a bike. It was even held at Le Mans between 1971 and 1977 and a second 24-hour race was actually established on the Le Mans Bugatti circuit after 1977 when the Bol D'Or moved on to Paul Ricard.

Like the Isle of Man TT, the Bol was originally a race for both cars and motorcycles, although the 'combined' running lasted far longer in the Bol D'Or. Bikes didn't get the event to themselves until the 1950s. Originally run in 1922 on a 3-mile clay track at Vaujours, the race has been held at several venues including Montlery and Paul Ricard, but since 2000 its home has been Magny-Cours, the home of the French Formula One Grand Prix from 1991 to 2008.

It is now part of the FIM Endurance Championship whose three main events are The Bol D'Or itself, the modern Le Mans 24-hour race and the 24 hours of Spa Francorchamps in Belgium.

Endurance racing of this type is largely a French (or at least francophone) pursuit, but there have been British successes, including a pair of wins for the Japauto team (themselves French) in both 1972 and 1973, using Honda engines fitted into Dresda frames designed and made by Dave Degens in West Sussex, and a victory for the Kawasaki mounted team of Terry Rymer, Carl Fogarty and Steve Hislop in 1992.

Mike Hailwood

Stanley Michael Bailey Hailwood MBE GM (Mike the Bike to his many fans) was born in April 1940 at Great Milton in Oxfordshire. His father was an ex-racer and motorcycle dealer, and like his peer John Surtees, Mike grew up in a biking atmosphere and learned to ride a motorcycle at an early age. Also like Surtees, he competed in both motorcycle and car racing at the highest levels, although the Formula One World Championship eluded him.

He worked for a short time in the family business before leaving to work for Triumph. He had his first race in 1957 at Oulton Park, soon after his seventeenth birthday. By 1961 Hailwood was racing for Honda, at that time a new name in motorcycling, and in June he became the first man in the history of the Isle of Man TT to win three races in one week, taking the 125cc, 250cc and 500cc events. He might

Mike Hailwood leading Phil Read into the Druids hairpin at Brands Hatch in the 1960s. (*Courtesy of Ron Coombs*)

have made it four had his 350cc AJS not broken a gudgeon pin while leading.

Hailwood won the 1961 250cc World Championship for Honda, but signed for MV Agusta in 1962, now becoming the first rider to win four consecutive 500cc World Championship titles during MV's remarkable years of dominance in the premier class. Returning to Honda, Hailwood won another four world titles in the smaller classes in 1966 and 1967.

The main production race of the season was the Hutchinson 100 at Silverstone and Mike won it in 1965 on a BSA Lightning, beating the Triumph team with their Bonnevilles. This was important to the manufacturers as production wins gave 'racing cred' to their current machines. The Triumphs were ridden by star riders Phil Read and Percy Tait, which illustrates the prestige in which the race was held. On this occasion it was pouring with rain, but Hailwood was lapping consistently above 80 mph, while top riders fell around him.

It was his heroic exploits at the TT which really made 'Mike the Bike' a household name. He won twelve TTs up to 1967, including a memorable Senior victory over Agostini in that year during which he raised the lap record to 108.77 mph. This would stand for eight years.

Honda took a temporary break from Grand Prix racing in 1968 and it is proof, if proof were needed, of the esteem in which they held Hailwood that they offered him a £50,000 retainer not to ride for other teams in their absence. However, with no factory able to compete with MV, he decided to try a move to car racing.

Although it is often stated that he failed to achieve the same level of success on four wheels as he had on two, this is not altogether fair. He won the European Formula Two Championship in 1972 in a Surtees, and ran at the front of the field in Formula 5000, a major international single-seater formula of the day. He achieved a third place finish in the Le Mans 24 Hours and he had a Formula One career lasting fifty races, scoring two podium finishes and amassing twenty-nine World Championship points. Not too shabby.

It was during this period of his life that Hailwood won the George Medal, the second highest award for bravery which is available to civilians in Britain. He went to the aid of Clay Regazzoni who was trapped in his burning and fuel-laden BRM following an accident on the second lap of the 1973 South African Grand Prix at Kyalami. Hailwood's overalls caught fire, but after being extinguished by the track marshals, he went back into the fire and rescued Regazzoni.

Hailwood's Formula One career ended when he was injured in the 1974 German Grand Prix, but in 1978 he announced his return to motorcycle racing and the Isle of Man. The general belief was that not even Mike the Bike could possibly succeed at the age of 38 and after an 11-year break from riding.

Riding a Ducati 900SS he won the Formula One TT and returned again in 1979 to win the Senior on a Suzuki RG500 two-stroke machine, bringing his career total to fourteen wins. He rode the same bike in the Unlimited Classic race and diced for the lead with Alex George throughout the entire six-lap distance, losing by two seconds after 226 miles.

Mike Hailwood was killed in 1981 in a road accident. A lorry turned into his path as he was driving to a chip shop with his children David and Michelle in the car. Michelle was killed instantly and Mike died in hospital. David escaped with minor injuries.

He was awarded the Segrave Trophy in 1979. He was recognised by the FIM as a 'Grand Prix Legend' in 2000 and inducted into the International Motorsports Hall of Fame in 2001. The AMA Motorcycle Hall of Fame admitted Mike Hailwood in 2000 and a section of the TT Mountain Circuit leading to the highest point is now known as Hailwood Rise. The highest point itself is named Hailwood's Height.

Speedway

Speedway is a specialised form of motorcycle racing. Four riders (or occasionally six) battle it out in a four-lap sprint anti-clockwise around an oval track surfaced with loose dirt or shale. The bikes use four-stroke single-cylinder 500cc engines, have no gears (or more correctly, a single gear) and no brakes. The fuel is pure methanol, which allows the engine to run with a greater compression ratio and gives more power. Speeds regularly exceed 70 mph and the riders slide their machines sideways through the turns.

There is debate about the precise origins of this style of competition. It has long been held that the first meeting was held in December 1923 in New South Wales, but not only is there evidence in contemporary newspaper reports that other similar events had already taken place in Australia, but that riders had been 'broadsiding' on dirt tracks in America before the First World War.

When you think about it, anyone with a motorcycle could have discovered how to slide it and many probably did. One of the Americans credited with inventing the technique is Don Johns, who was said to be able to ride an oval track with the throttle wide open all the way round. The racing was called 'short track racing', but it was essentially Speedway.

Colin Watson, Alf Medcalf and 'Digger' Pugh demonstrated the art in the UK in April 1928, but dirt track races are thought to have been held at Camberley, Surrey, and Droylsden, Manchester, before this date. What is clear is that the first professional Speedway meeting on British soil took place at Celtic Park on 28 April 1928, and that the popularity of the sport in the 1920s was amazing. It caught the public imagination to such an extent that the organisers of meetings could scarcely accommodate – or predict – the crowds of spectators arriving at their gates. There were occasions when as many as 20,000 people turned out.

Of course, there was money to be made from this popularity, both for the organisers of meetings and also for the riders who provided the thrills and spills. What's more, following the introduction of the British Speedway League in 1930, even though the sport had many of its origins in Australia and most of the best riders were Aussies, the biggest money was in England. At a time when the average wage in Australia was around $6 per week, a top rider could earn the equivalent of $200 per night and race seven nights a week. The great Australian rider Vic Huxley once earned more than £5,000 (about $10,000) in a single year racing for Wimbledon. Unsurprisingly, there was a flood of good Aussie riders queuing to ride for British clubs.

Fay Taylour

Fay Taylour (1904-83) was one of those remarkable women who ride faster and better than the vast majority of their male counterparts. In fact, throughout the short history of motorcycling, the machines have attracted those whose individuality makes them stand out from the crowd; Fay was certainly unique. As a dirt track and Speedway rider she faced hostility not only from some of the men, but even from the rule makers. Most Speedway organisers were simply unwilling to let a woman ride, and she was only able to demonstrate her ability when the officials at the Crystal Palace track were away on the Isle of Man for the TT. Amazing how that one event has had so much influence – even by simply distracting attention away from a Speedway venue! By the time they came back she had done enough to prove that she could ride a Speedway bike.

Having raced successfully at Crystal Palace, she toured Australia and set the fastest time at more than one meeting. When she returned she found that women had been officially banned from all British Speedway tracks. So no more Speedway, but that didn't stop her competing in Trials events on a powerful and heavy 500cc Panther, or going to America and racing 'Midgets' on the short circuits.

Although few have heard of her today, Fay Taylour was one of Britain's most famous motorcyclists in the 1920s. Her reputation was harmed during the Second World War when her known friendship with Sir Oswald Mosley resulted in her being interned – ironically, in the Isle of Man – but after living and racing cars for a few years in America after the War, she returned to live in England in 1953.

The Maudes Trophy

Speed has not always been the only factor which makers need to demonstrate, however, as the buying public have naturally always wanted reliability and ease of handling. In fact, most bikes have always been sold for purposes such as commuting, for which speed is not even a consideration. Events to test machines' agility, reliability and toughness therefore developed alongside out-and-out races. Trials demonstrate agility, and endurance events show that machines can run without problems over long distances.

The Maudes Trophy is awarded directly to the manufacturer for outstanding performances. The trophy was initially donated in 1923 by George Pettyt, of the Maudes Motor Mart and he stipulated that it must be competed for under impartially observed conditions, and that the bikes must be standard showroom models. The Auto Cycle Union (ACU) provided the impartial observation and has awarded the trophy ever since, but only in years when it is considered that a suitably impressive achievement has occurred.

It was first awarded in 1923 to Norton, and most recently in 1994 when a team of ten New Zealanders averaged over 100 mph on Yamaha FZR 600 machines (known as the YZF 600 in the USA) during the Junior Isle of Man TT. In between, the trophy has been won by many of the British makers featured in this story.

Trials Riding

Trials riding has produced its own 'greats'. Marjorie Cottle was considered one of Britain's best riders in the 1920s, while the exploits of Sammy Miller on his 500cc Ariel HT5 made even its number plate (GOV 132) famous. In later years the Lampkin dynasty have continued this tradition.

As early as the 1920s, trials events diversified in Britain into a new form of racing over rough ground which came to be known as 'scrambling'. This is now an international sport in its own right and is now called motocross; the name deriving from the French word 'motocyclette' and 'cross country'.

Of course pure racing on tarmac has always been a major draw with its combination of speed and danger. Whether on the great banked circuits such as Brooklands in England or Montlhéry in France or on the many shorter tracks which exist in most parts of the world, every kind of machine from Bantams to Superbikes is raced. The FIM World Championship (MotoGP) is seen by many as the pinnacle and riders such as Lorenzo, Pedrosa and Stoner are household names even as Handley, Duke, Ivy and Hailwood were in their day.

Chapter 4

Some More Big Names

Brough Superior

George Brough was the son of a motorcycle manufacturer, and at the end of the First World War he built himself his own 'ideal' motorcycle. His father was not impressed and George decided to take his £1,000 share out of the family business and set up his own works. He called his machines the Brough Superior (at the suggestion of a friend in a pub!) to distinguish them from his father's, and it is perhaps not too surprising that Brough senior was not impressed by this either! 'I suppose that makes mine the Brough Inferior' is said to have been his response. Nevertheless they seem to have remained on good terms as the first three or four Superiors were built by George and his assistant Ike Webb in the elder Mr Brough's house while the new works were being prepared.

It is in fact likely that the father was a better engineer than the son, since he built his own successful engines; something George never did. George Brough's machines were powered by engines from Matchless, JAP and very occasionally other sources. Yet his fame and influence were enormous, despite his decision that each machine be hand-crafted, limiting the number which could be made. In all, only about 3,000 Brough Superior motorcycles left the works – a tiny total in mass production terms.

These machines matched their manufacturer-guaranteed straight-line performance with state-of-the-art handling, winning numerous major races including four consecutive victories in the Welsh TT at Pendine Sands. When the trophy went missing in the late 1920s there were even rumours (later to be proved unfounded) that George Brough's manservant might have made off with it.

The Brough was not sold as a racing machine though. It was simply intended to be the best motorcycle money could buy. The Brough Superior was marketed as the 'Rolls Royce of Motorcycles'. This title was one of those things which a manufacturer must dream of. It arose when H. D. Teague, Midland editor of *The Motorcycle*, having road tested the SS80 model, used the phrase in summing up his impressions. George Brough, who personally wrote all his advertising copy, used the accolade in every subsequent advert and in every catalogue. Of course he was always careful to attribute it to *The Motorcycle*!

No two bikes were exactly the same, since it was part of George Brough's philosophy that the Rolls Royce of Motorcycles should be built individually to match the customer's precise requirements.

A consequence of the bikes' individual specifications was a tendency for them to receive nicknames from their owners. George Brough's own 1922 SS80 racer, though originally referred to disparagingly by his competitors as *Spit and Polish* because of its immaculate presentation, came to be known to him as *Old Bill* after a well-known cartoon character of the time.

The SS100 model was developed after the SS80. Bert LeVack had improved the Val Page-designed 8/45 overhead valve JAP engine to the extent that he had pushed the World Record speed to 119 mph and George Brough had ensured that his name was on the tank – although little else appears to have come from his works.

Brough saw the opportunity to produce a road bike which would safely top 100 mph. It had to have the power of the Page/LeVack JAP engine and it also had to handle well. By 1925 when George Brough released it to the public (or at least to the few who could afford it) it handled superbly and looked superb as well. These were the looks that defined every subsequent Brough Superior.

T. E. Lawrence (Lawrence of Arabia) was a regular Brough customer, buying a new machine each year, and in a remarkable letter sent to George Brough in 1927 he wrote: 'I'm not a speed merchant, but ride fairly far in the day (occasionally 700 miles, often 500) ... The riding position and the slow powerful turn-over of the engine at speeds of 50 odd, give one a very restful feeling.'

How many of us would ride that far in a day today, on smooth roads and modern machines? Brough naturally used this letter from one of the day's greatest celebrities (and heroes) in his advertising.

T. E. Lawrence owned seven Brough Superiors and his love of them provided an advertising opportunity which GB was far too shrewd to miss.

Above and below: The Brough Superior SS100. A fabulous JAP V-twin giving a guaranteed ability to reach 100 mph and a massive speedometer to leave the rider in no doubt.

Lawrence called his machines *Boa*, short for Boanerges, a name derived from the Greek form of 'Sons of Thunder', the name given by Jesus to the brothers James and John. His second and subsequent machines were also named *George*, possibly after their designer, but as he replaced them he made them altogether more regal by adding numbers. *George VIII* was never delivered as it was still under construction at the works when, on 19 May 1935, Lawrence tragically died of injuries he had received six days previously while riding *George VII*.

Lawrence was a hugely enthusiastic motorcyclist and his riding sometimes showed that same fearlessness which had previously won him renown in war. He may have claimed not to be a 'speed merchant' but it is scarcely possible to read his own description of his 1925 race with a Bristol fighter aircraft (which he won comfortably) without feeling that he still possessed that implacable disregard for his own safety which wins both races and medals.

He rode without helmet or goggles, screwing up his eyes against the wind in order to see, at speeds of around 100 mph and feeling flies hitting his face 'like spent bullets'. He leapt over crests and grounded so fiercely that the mudguards touched the tyres and he survived a tank-slapping weave which gave him 'thirty awful yards'.

He even reduced speed for a time to let the pilot think he could win and also admitted that at one point he almost frightened an oncoming driver into the ditch. Then he continued on to Lincoln, Newark and Sleaford on his way back to his base, the RAF college at Cranwell. Along the way he bought bacon, eggs, sausages and dripping; he made this journey twice a week for months, ostensibly just to buy the best food cheaply!

His love of the Brough and its JAP engine (which he reckoned would travel to the moon without faltering) was such that he even liked to imagine it returned his feelings and gave him 5 mph more than another rider would receive.

It is often overlooked that in addition to building the best motorcycles money could buy and writing effective advertising copy, George Brough was also a very fine rider. *Old Bill* was built as a racer for his personal use in 1922 and was almost certainly the best turned-out racer at Brooklands until Bill Lacey started nickel plating his bikes.

Despite the ribbing Brough suffered at the hands of the owners of less pampered bikes, he won on the bike's debut, achieving the first win and the first 100-mph lap by a side valve machine into the bargain. Unfortunately the front tyre left the rim at full throttle in another race later the same day and the resulting high-speed crash left George in hospital.

On his recovery, he rebuilt the machine with a 976cc 'KTR' JAP V-twin personally tuned by Bert LeVack, which had been lightened to the extent that the flywheel had been reduced to a single 'spoke' and an outer rim. The bike also received additional frame struts on account of the special engine, a new fork and its nickname at this time.

Over the next year or two, George and *Bill* won fifty-one sprint events together (beating George Dance, the most famous sprint rider of the day on numerous occasions) before crashing again at Clipstone in Nottinghamshire. *Bill* did cross the finishing line on this occasion but George was no longer on board. This time when

George returned from hospital following a number of skin grafts his racing days were done. *Old Bill* was returned to road trim.

During the Second World War, the bike was put into store but was damaged rather bizarrely when a cast iron bath fell through a ceiling and landed on it ...

After the War it was bought by Titch Allen, the founder of the Vintage Motor Cycle Club and restored to 1922 specification with the help of, among others, George Brough himself.

Brough did not rest on his laurels after the development of the SS100. That was never his way. He continued to feel that the perfect motorcycle was waiting to be designed and that his firm ought to lead the way. His view – held by many in the 1920s – seems to have been that the ideal motorcycle would have the silence and refinement of a car. This led him to believe that it would have four cylinders and shaft drive. Those who knew him always felt that his first love was in fact the joy and power of the big V-twin, but he continued to attempt to build the 'ideal' bike just the same.

There were several of these four-cylinder machines; an in-line Vee, a straight four, a shaft-driven design with twin rear wheels powered by an Austin car engine and a horizontally opposed four. This last was intended as a sidecar machine, but of the ten built at least two saw solo service. None of the four-cylinder bikes was commercially successful and they cost a great deal of money to produce, but they created a stir in the Shows of 1927, 1928, 1931 and 1932 and their publicity value was immense.

Brough's final show-stopping four-cylinder design was the Golden Dream of 1938. This was intended to be the ultimate Brough Superior and effectively used a pair of

The Brough damper requires no tools for its adjustment.

The 1,000cc JAP V-twin fitted to the Brough Superior known as *Moby Dick*.

horizontally opposed twins built as a unit one above the other and geared together to form an H4 engine, although Brough called it a 'flat vertical' configuration.

The movements of pistons and camshafts were arranged such that all vibrations from the pistons and all gyroscopic effects from the camshafts were cancelled out. It was intended to be as near as humanly possible a completely vibrationless engine. Bore and stroke of 68 x 68 mm kept it compact. The frame departed from normal Brough practice by using plunger rear suspension in conjunction with the underslung worm drive from the drive shaft.

Five Golden Dreams were built in 1939, but when the Second World War came, Brough production was switched to the manufacture of components for Rolls Royce.

It was estimated that putting the Dream on the market after the war would have cost at least £80,000 and materials could only be obtained if a permit was obtained from the government. This would have required a guarantee from Brough of adequate export business and it was clear that there was little market for such expensive luxury motorcycles. It was, sadly, the end of George Brough's era.

The Brough Superior SS100 illustrated, nicknamed *Moby Dick*, is interesting in a number of ways. It is fitted with a JAP 1,142cc V-twin engine and a Norton four-speed foot-change gearbox. The engine is original, though modified early in its life, but the bike was fitted with a Sturmey-Archer three-speed gearbox when new. This was hand operated and many owners made the upgrade to the Norton box. In its original three-speed form the bike was tested by *Motor Cycling* magazine in 1931 and achieved a top speed of 106 mph (all SS100 and SS80 models were certified by the factory as being capable of at least 100 mph and 80 mph respectively). With more tuning work carried out, *Moby Dick* later reached 115 mph – and 109 mph in second gear!

Opinions vary concerning the plated frame. Some (presumably including all those who bid huge sums for it!) consider it magnificent. Others regard it as over the top. You pays your money and you takes your choice. If you've got enough money of course...

When sold at auction by Bonhams in October 2011, the bike fetched £210,500 and became one of the top ten most expensive motorcycles in the world. Its exact position in the list depends on the currency used in the calculation and the current exchange rate.

Vincent

Chief among those who rejected the telescopic fork were Phil Vincent and his long-time chief engineer Phil Irving. Vincent had bought the remnants (essentially the name) of the unprofitable HRD Motors Ltd in 1928 and renamed it Vincent HRD Co. Ltd. Irving joined him in 1931.

Vincent motorcycles are legendary. This author first encountered one (a Black Shadow) while learning to ride on the excellent RAC/ACU Training scheme in the early 1970s. One of the instructors rode in on this amazing, huge – to my inexperienced eyes – black monster. For me, ever since, there has been something 'serious' about a 1,000cc V-twin, but nothing quite like a Vincent with its slow thump ('one bang per telegraph pole' was the joke) and those 'old-fashioned' girder forks which never quite looked 'right' to a youngster ... My tastes have improved since.

To me, still wobbling around on a BSA Bantam and finding its limited power quite adequate to be going on with, the Vincent looked and sounded like a 'proper man's bike'. Yes I know – and indeed I could name – several women who ride much better than I ever will, but it's how I felt just the same.

The V-twin engine was designed by Phil Irving, an Australian who went on to design the World Championship winning Repco Formula One engines used by Brabham in the mid-1960s. It took the arrival of the Cosworth DFV/Lotus 49/Jim Clark combination in 1967 to push them off the top of the heap.

There is a story that Irving came up with the idea of the Vee when he accidentally placed two tracings of the existing 500cc Vincent single on top of each other, with one back to front. He noticed that by carefully arranging them he could arrive at a workable layout for a 1,000cc V-twin. The idea of a V-twin engine as a pair of singles on a common crank was certainly far from new, and personally I see no reason to doubt that he did it deliberately. Actually, the Cosworth DFV (Double Four Valve)

was designed in a similar (and deliberate) way, combining two 1,600cc FVA heads to make a 3-litre V8.

The V-twin was so strongly built that it enabled Vincent to take another revolutionary step in design by using it as a stressed structural component of the bike. Many of the tubes used in a conventional frame were eliminated and the overall result was extremely rigid. Interestingly, this also finds an exact parallel in the 1967 Lotus 49.

I had the good fortune to meet both the son-in-law and the grandson of Phil Vincent along with restorer and owner-of-Vincents Bill Bewley on the Isle of Man in 2011. Bill told me many interesting things (such as how to recognise instantly whether a Vincent still has its original engine) while Robin told me of his father-in-law's long-term unfulfilled desire to build a ceramic engine as he so disliked seeing heat going to waste.

Series 'C' and 'D' Vincents from 1948 onwards were fitted with hydraulic dampers and their forks were described as 'Girdraulic'. This fork can be seen clearly in the photograph of a 1948 Black Lightning. This was a stripped down racing version of the 998cc Black Shadow. Many steel parts were replaced with aluminium or removed altogether. Note the aluminium wheel rims, the racing seat, the lack of lights and the rearset racing footrests.

The Vincent's reputation as the fastest production motorcycle was enhanced on 13 September 1948 at Bonneville Salt Flats when Rollie Free set a motorcycle Land Speed Record of 150.313 mph. He rode a Black Lightning, lying flat on the rear mudguard with his legs straight out behind him, the seat having been removed. To further reduce drag, Free wore only a pair of swimming trunks and a pair of 'sneakers'. There is clearly some kind of headgear visible in the picture (over the page) and some sources refer to this as a shower cap, but it actually looks like the 'pudding basin' helmet Free normally wore. It could only have served to reduce wind resistance in any case – if he had come off the bike he would have been skinned alive.

Although many Vincent owners place a high value on the originality of their bikes, there have been a number of 'special projects' based on them over the years. These include out and out racers, show specials and even a few intended for limited production. Fritz Egli is a Swiss frame designer and former racer whose 'Egli-Vincent' caused a stir in the '60s and '70s. Today, Patrick Godet builds these machines in France and his beautiful 'Red Shadow' is pictured on p. 57 at the Vintage Motor cycle Club's Manx Grand Prix festival in 2011.

Opposite above: This 1938 A-Series HRD-Vincent Comet was donated to the Vincent Owners Club by Nigel Seymour-Smith. It is rotated around the sections on an annual basis and members draw lots for riding privileges. Brian Wigmore of the Mid-Gloucestershire section was understandably delighted to have the use of the bike, which is a 'special' with a bronze cylinder head, for the 2012 Manx Grand Prix Festival. Being an early machine, it is fitted with a conventional girder fork.

Opposite below: The Vincent Black Lightning is a stripped down racing version of the Black Shadow, fitted with the later Vincent 'Girdraulic' fork. It was a bike similar to this one which was ridden by Rollie Free at Bonneville, though he took the stripping further than most....

Opposite above: Phil Irving's impressively massive looking V-Twin engine in the Black Shadow.

Opposite below: 150 mph on salt. Free later said he would have ridden standing up if it would have made it go faster.

Above: A gorgeous Egli-Vincent Red Shadow by Patrick Godet graces Tony East's front lawn.

Right: The rare 'Grey Shadow' is started before an exhibition run.

Royal Enfield

And now to what some claim to be the oldest surviving motorcycle manufacturer anywhere – though others argue that the Les Harris Triumph Bonneville, produced for five years in the 1980s, represents 'continuity of production' and therefore entitles Triumph to the honour.

In 1851 George Townsend set up a needle making business in Hunt End, near Redditch in Worcestershire. His son, George Junior, followed the path we have seen before; he began to make parts for bicycles and even invented and patented a new form of saddle.

By 1890 the firm was in financial trouble. Townsend left, but the company's fortunes were revived by a contract to supply rifle parts to the Royal Small Arms Factory in Enfield, Middlesex, and the name was changed to The Royal Enfield Manufacturing Co. Ltd soon afterwards.

The first powered vehicle from the factory was a car with a De Dion engine which rolled out in 1898, but a motorcycle followed in 1901. This had a 150cc engine fitted above the front wheel, and by the start of the First World War, Enfield were building some very smart-looking bikes with V-twin JAP engines.

With the onset of war, Enfield was contracted to supply motorcycles to the forces. Their sidecar outfits were fitted to carry machine guns into battle. There was also a stretcher-bearing version and Enfield started producing its own engines – although they were still fitting JAPs in some models several years later.

By the mid-1920s there were Enfield machines with two- and four-stroke engines and sidecar outfits. This range, with solid build quality and modern appearance, continued to sell through the hardships of the 1930s.

The Second World War again saw Royal Enfield machines ordered in great numbers and this time they included the 'Flying Flea', a 125cc machine that looked rather like a miniature BSA Bantam. Not surprising perhaps, since like the Bantam, it was developed from a DKW design!

The Flea was designed to be dropped from an aircraft along with airborne troops, thus allowing them to move quickly on the ground. For this purpose it was supplied with its own parachute and a 'birdcage' structure to protect it on landing.

However, the most famous model name associated with Royal Enfield is the 'Bullet'. The first Bullet was a single-cylinder machine, introduced in 1931. This Bullet featured exposed valves and was made in both 350cc and 500cc options.

The 1933 250cc Bullet was quite different, having a girder fork, saddle tank and a solid rear end. The bike achieved its present-day form in 1949 with a 350cc

Opposite and next page: The Royal Enfield Bullet in its not-so-varied forms. A ten-year-old 500cc Scrambler has extra ground clearance, knobbly tyres and single seat. A much older road bike carries a few everyday 'accoutrements'. The latest model is equipped with full modern electrics. The additional lever behind the kickstarter is a neutral selector. Apparently it also functions as a gear indicator, but of course you'd have to stop and get off to use it. Most other machines manage quite well with just a neutral light.

single-cylinder engine, telescopic forks and swinging arm rear suspension. The 350cc machine's strong engine made it a successful trials bike; success which increased further with the appearance of a 500cc alternative in 1953.

In 1954 the Indian government placed an order for 800 Bullets. This stretched the factory to its limit and when similar orders arrived in 1955 and 1956 the decision was made to set up a factory in India. The workers were trained in Redditch to produce the 1955 Bullet and, in effect, they continued to do so for many years. Enfield India Ltd, who now own the rights to the Royal Enfield name, have responded to developments in materials and manufacturing over the years and have sometimes been forced to change the bikes in the face of legislation, but they have retained the look and feel of the Bullet their customers love. Only in very recent times has a Unit Construction engine and gearbox been introduced with five gears and the gear lever moved to the left side of the machine. The Bullet Standard 350 ceased production for the European market in 2007 due to ever more stringent emission laws, but the new lean-burn all-aluminium Unit Construction engines have ensured that the Royal Enfield Bullet, which has been exported in vast numbers to at least twenty countries, should remain on the scene for a long time yet. You can even still get it with a sidecar. But it isn't made in Redditch. Times change ...

Velocette

Velocette motorcycles are among the most highly regarded of classic British machinery. The family-run company was always small compared to the likes of BSA and Triumph and production was correspondingly limited, yet at any modern meeting of classic bike enthusiasts the Velocette is always well represented.

The firm was founded by Johannes Gutgemann, who was born in the town of Oberwinter in the German Rhineland around the middle of the nineteenth century. Gutgemann moved to England at the age of 19 with his Birmingham-born wife Elizabeth. The couple, not unnaturally, chose to start their new life in her home city and Johannes gained a partnership in the firm of Isaac Taylor and Company, making bicycles and fittings. At this point he took the name of John Taylor and soon after took British citizenship. It was later, in 1917, that John Taylor formally adopted an anglicised version of his original name and became John Goodman.

After one or two 'ups and downs' in the world of business, Taylor, now in partnership with William Gue, created a motorcycle in 1905. They named the 2-hp machine the Veloce, this being an Italian term used as a direction in music and meaning 'to be played rapidly'. The bike was not a commercial success and later the same year Taylor Gue was wound up. Taylor now set up a new company, using the name Veloce Limited. His first premises were in Fleet Street, Birmingham. Veloce didn't make the move south to their more famous factory in Hall Green (via a short stay in Aston) until 1926.

The company's first bikes were again named 'Veloce', but real success only came with the introduction of a range of lightweight two-strokes, which being small bikes,

This very basic two-stroke Model A was one of the first Veloce machines to carry the 'Velocette' name which was to become the company's world famous identity. (*Courtesy of Paul D'Orleans/ The Vintagent*)

were called Velocettes. This name became familiar to the buying public and it stuck, even after the firm later returned to producing four-strokes.

By 1907 Taylor's two sons, Percy and Eugene, were also in business, encouraged by their father and trading under the name New Veloce Motors. They had intended to manufacture cars but never achieved full production, so instead, their father commissioned engines from them for a 276cc 2½-hp four-stroke motorcycle which reached prototype form in 1909. This had many innovative features, but did not sell well, so in 1910 it was joined by a less advanced 499cc side-valve model. Sales of the smaller machine did eventually pick up in 1912 and now a ladies version was added. Soon a pair of two-speed chain driven models (for gentlemen and ladies) and a Veloce sidecar had all joined the growing range.

When New Veloce failed the two sons joined John Goodman's business and the first of the Velocette two-strokes, a 206cc model, made its appearance in 1913. This bike was so well received by the public that by the end of the decade Veloce were only making Velocettes; clutches and electric lights were added along the way. The two-speed belt-drive Model A and chain drive Model B were manufactured from 1924 as economy machines.

Four-stroke motorcycles finally made a comeback to the range in 1925 with the

This pre-war KTT may have gained a more modern set of wheels but it retains all of its original sense of racing purpose.

Model K. Apparently the 'K' could have stood for 'camshaft' and if so it is perhaps a reflection in spelling of the family's German origins (although the German for camshaft is actually nockenwelle). This 350cc overhead camshaft machine was the first of a long-lasting line; the first of the classic Velocettes. It was briefly called a Veloce, but this error was soon rectified and the goodwill earned by the two-strokes was not squandered.

Accurate engine timing was achieved by the use of a strobe light which enabled the engine to be studied in motion. This technique is taken for granted in engineering today (although modern electronically controlled engines require more complex equipment), but it was pioneered in the automotive setting by Veloce.

There were some early teething troubles with the engine, but after a year or so the Super Sport KSS version was ready to be entered in competition and the KTT was prepared specifically for the Isle of Man. Alec Bennett won Velocette's first TT in 1926 – by the enormous margin of ten minutes.

As development progressed the machine became the first Junior bike to lap the Mountain Circuit at more than 70 mph and won a number of TT and Manx Grand Prix races. It also set a new 350cc record of 100.39 mph at Brooklands.

The KTT was the first motorcycle to be fitted with a positive stop foot gearchange, i.e. one that could change up or down with a single click. This proved to be an

From 1948 the 350cc Velocette MAC gained telescopic forks at the front, but it had to wait until 1953 for a swinging arm rear. The bike pictured dates from around 1951.

advantage not only in racing but on the road, rapidly making the awkward hand operated gear levers obsolete. The Velocette system remains the standard on virtually all motorbikes even today.

The K series machines required a degree of hand building, particularly of the shaft and bevel camshaft drive, and this increased production costs. In 1933, the company decided to develop a more affordable model, and the result was the 'M' series.

The MOV was based on a 250cc engine of 'square' design, meaning that the bore and stroke were equal at 68 mm. Its camshaft drive was simpler than the Model K and required less skilled labour to assemble. This bike was an immediate success, and when the stroke was lengthened to increase its capacity to 350cc the 'MAC' version sold even better. Both proved reliable, quick and well-mannered, and brought much needed capital into the firm.

One interesting Velocette customer was Graham Hill, later to be Formula One World Champion and father of World Champion Damon. Graham's motor sport career began in 1948 when, aged 19, he did a small amount of motorcycle scrambling (now called motocross) on a 350cc Velocette. He didn't even learn to drive a car until almost five years later. Hill's mother had in fact ridden a Triumph 250 from the age of 17.

The 500cc Velocette MSS of 1935 onward was again popular and profitable. It was a completely new machine, though its design was clearly based on earlier bikes, the frame being developed from the Mk V KTT racer but made stronger and heavier so that the MSS would be suitable for sidecar use.

Not even a brief discussion of Velocette history could be complete without mention

The ever-popular Velocette MSS (slightly less sporty brother of the Venom) with the marque's distinctive 'map of Africa' timing cover.

A particularly smart Venom Thruxton with its rear-set footrests (note the extension link between the gear lever and the gearbox), alloy wheels, larger tank and carburettor, lower bars and single seat.

of the Venom. This 500cc machine was produced from 1955 to 1970. Launched at the same time as the Viper, the single-cylinder Venom was a development of the MSS and was sold in direct competition with the full line up of great British twins. It therefore flew in the face of the design ideas of men such as Edward Turner, but of course Eugene Goodman, who had come up with the idea of the Venom, knew a thing or two as well. Many enthusiasts, then as now, retained a love of the steady pulsing beat of a big single, and there was room in the marketplace for a good one.

The Venom's engine had a cast-iron cylinder liner, a high compression ratio and a light alloy head. The layout of the timing mechanism and head enabled the push rods to be kept short, enabling efficient valve operation, but at much lower cost than an overhead cam design.

An interesting feature of the Venom, which can be seen clearly in the photos, is a method of mounting rear shock absorbers which allows the damping and spring rates to be adjusted easily by the owner. The upper mounting point is elongated and the top end of the spring/damper unit can be moved along the slot. Towards the vertical gives stiffer springing and more damping; away from the vertical has the opposite effect. The stiffer settings are particularly useful when carrying a passenger on the pillion.

The Venom was, from the start, a handsome bike with excellent performance and a very good standard of finish. The chrome was (and is) of top quality and the black paintwork with gold pin striping not only looked smart when new, but was intended to stay smart.

A special 'Thruxton' variant was introduced in 1965 and was Bertie Goodman's final development of the Velocette. The Thruxton had rear-set footrests, a close ratio four-speed gearbox, alloy rims, a duplex front brake, a race specification large valve head and clip-on handlebars. Its Amal carburettor (*see Glossary*) was so big that even the fuel tank had to be modified to make room for it. It produced 41 bhp, five more than the Venom.

The bike was clearly very much a racer intended to be used in races such as the Thruxton 500, which gave it its name, but these events were open to production machines only. The answer was of course to market the Thruxton as a road bike; over 1,100 were eventually made. Many others have been produced by owners upgrading Venoms since. In effect, the Thruxton is a factory-made café racer.

One of the most remarkable feats in motorcycling history was performed by a Velocette Venom; covering 2,400 miles in 24 hours, thereby averaging over 100 mph, on the high-speed banked circuit at Montlhéry in France. The record bike was not tuned as such, although a fairing was fitted and unnecessary road fittings such as mudguards, lights (!) and speedometer were removed. It was tested by Bertie Goodman who was not only the grandson of John Goodman, the son of Percy Goodman and the Managing Director of the company, but also a hugely experienced and enthusiastic motorcyclist. Goodman tested the Venom at the Motor Industry Research Association test track, running for 14 hours at full throttle, just before the bike was taken to France. It is said that the engine was not stripped down in between.

Much of the organisational work for the record attempt was done by French racing champion Georges Monneret (who had originally suggested the idea to Goodman)

Velocette were justifiably proud of their racing successes.

and his son Pierre. They arranged for a team of French riders, but the actual selection was not made until the night before. The selection criterion was simple. If you can dare to keep the throttle pegged to maximum without 'lifting' at all you are in. One who made it into the team was Managing Director Bertie Goodman.

As at Brooklands, the bankings at Montlhéry were horribly bumpy even though the actual concrete was better supported and more stable. There were expansion joints every few metres and these were inches wide in places There was also no lighting and so 12-volt headlamps were set up, but of course these only provided 'stripes' of light which caused fatigue, dizziness and even hallucinations.

This sustained speed on an overhead-valve single has never been equalled since. Some of the riders ran only fifteen minute stints due to fatigue, but 42-year-old Goodman insisted on taking full one-hour turns throughout. A truly heroic performance.

The board at Veloce were always regular riders, not only of motorcycles, but of their company's motorcycles. This alone set them apart from virtually all of their competitors and it showed in the nature and quality of Velocette machines. They are true riders' bikes. Always heavily involved in competition, and always well towards the front, their greatest milestones along with the 24-hour record were back-to-back 350cc World Championships in 1949-1950 for Freddie Frith and Bob Foster.

It must be pointed out that in spite of all the beautiful and successful models described above, there was another famous machine made by Veloce Ltd. The relatively humble 192cc Velocette LE (Little Engine) was actually the best-selling

Velocette model of all. It sold to police forces in great numbers and earned the title 'noddy bike'. Opinions vary on the reason for this. Many believe that it is a reference to Enid Blyton's character who was often in trouble with Mr Plod, but there is a strong and plausible story that the term arises from the police themselves. Constables were instructed not to salute sergeants and officers when riding motorcycles, but simply to nod as this was obviously safer!

Sadly, the production costs of the LE were high and it was never truly profitable, though it remained in the catalogue for nearly 20 years. The Viceroy scooter on the other hand was never a success. It was perhaps aimed at a market which the keen motorcyclist Bertie Goodman didn't really understand. Be that as it may, the market rejected it and only about 700 were made. A sizeable loan taken out to finance development of the scooter remained largely outstanding when the Veloce company went into liquidation in 1971, their main products having become too dated to compete with the fresh new Japanese imports.

Chapter 5

Innovations, Good Sense – and a Few False Starts

Greeves

The story goes that Bert Greeves, whose cousin Derek (Derry) Preston Cobb was disabled, was mowing his lawn one day when he had an idea. The engine in his lawnmower could be used to power his cousin's wheelchair. This may be apocryphal, given that various powered invalid carriages had existed in various forms since at least 1922, but Greeves and Cobb worked together to design what came to be known as the 'Invacar'.

The fibreglass-bodied and invariably blue Invacar had three wheels and was powered by a small Villiers engine, until Villiers engine supply ceased in the early 1970s, and then by Steyr-Puch 500cc and 600cc units.

In 1952 Greeves won a contract to supply these little three-wheeled vehicles to the government's Ministry of Pensions. The cars were not sold to their disabled 'owners'. Instead the Ministry retained ownership and leased the cars to disabled drivers as required. The cars, in spite of certain disadvantages, not least the inevitable stigma which some drivers felt they generated, were generally considered a success for a great many years, giving mobility to a large number of those who might otherwise have been housebound. They remained in production until the contract was finally ended in 1977.

In reality there can be no doubt that by 1977 the single-seat design was terribly outdated. Even one of the firm's senior testers admitted later that a gust of wind would try to force the car off the road or into the path of an oncoming vehicle! This apparently didn't stop the workforce 'borrowing' test vehicles overnight on trade plates to go home in though....

Derry Preston Cobb himself had a renowned sense of humour and is reported to have modified his 'powered wheelchair' by fitting it with a 250cc racing engine. It could occasionally be seen to do an estimated 80 mph, and on odd occasions when he rolled it over he would simply wait there laughing for someone to come along and push it upright.

When the end came it was simply because the design of mainstream cars had moved on so far. Motorists who had earlier moved on from sidecar combinations to Minis were now moving on again to the Ford Capri and Vauxhall Viva. It was time for the disabled driver to move on too, but it took concerted protests to make it happen. The drivers' protests were backed by high profile figures including Graham Hill. Hill was asked to drive an Invacar and in 1974 he was quoted in the House of Lords by Baroness Phillips as follows:

> I was so appalled at what I found that ever since then I have tried everything within my power to publicise the fact that such vehicles should not be allowed on the road.

The Motability scheme, which began in 1978, replaced the blue trikes, allowing disabled drivers access to modified conventional cars. This was not actually the end for the Invacar, of course, as many were still in use – and there were drivers who loved them. The final compulsory recall and scrapping did not occur until April 2003. Soon after the cars were recalled, their end was finalised by a change in the law making it illegal to use them on the public highway.

It is not the Invacar which accounts for Bert Greeves' appearance in this book, of course. He had been a motorcycle enthusiast from his youth and in 1951, at the age of 45, he began to think about making them; production began two years later at his factory in Thundersley, Essex.

He used an unconventional but effective suspension system, based directly on the rubber-in-torsion springing he had already used in the Invacar, several years ahead of Isigonis' use of rubber suspension in the Mini. The front forks were of a leading link

This Triumph-engined scrambler illustrates the 'banana' version of the Greeves leading link fork, though this one uses conventional telescopic damper units.

type, but the pivot carried rubber-in-torsion spring units. Later versions in which the fork stanchion curved backwards to the pivot point became known as 'Banana' forks. In what could be seen as a gesture towards a slightly earlier age, damping was by manually adjustable friction discs.

The frame was unlike any other bike of its day in having the steering head and the large front down member combined in a cast alloy H-section beam. Greeves had added a foundry to the factory to produce these and it would be many years before the frame castings were replaced by a Reynolds 531 downtube (*see Glossary*). Conventional Ceriani forks which gave much greater suspension travel were available as an option on 'Challenger' models from 1966. Alloy cast frames are of course virtually universal on bikes with sporting credentials nowadays; Bert Greeves was not afraid to be ahead of his time when he saw a good reason to be. Greeves motorcycles were always light and powered by small engines, but they proved themselves able to embarrass many of the giants of the industry in trials and scrambles.

In 1957 Greeves took on Brian Stonebridge, previously a BSA works rider; he rode a 200cc Greeves to second place in a 500cc race at Hawkstone Park, in which the big manufacturers were represented by top riders on large factory machines. Some believe that this was the beginning of the end for large-engined bikes in what was even then becoming the truly international sport we know today.

Stonebridge was appointed Competition Manager and Development Engineer at Greeves, as he was a talented two-stroke tuning specialist and was able to improve significantly the performance of the Villiers engines. He also finished second in the 1959 FIM 250cc European Motocross Championship and would presumably have gone on to assist further in establishing Greeves' reputation, but he was sadly killed in a road accident in October 1959. He and Bert Greeves were returning from a visit to a factory in Bradford when they were in a head-on collision. Bert escaped with minor injuries but Stonebridge died at the scene.

Following the death of Brian Stonebridge Greeves signed Dave Bickers who won both the 1960 and 1961 250cc European Championships, while another young man, Bill Wilkinson, won the 1960 British Experts Trial on a Greeves machine with his 'L' plates attached! This was the first time the event had ever been won by a rider on a two-stroke motorcycle.

By 1962 the Greeves range had swollen to eleven models, of which four were roadsters. It is perhaps no great surprise that Greeves made a successful entry into road racing with the 250cc Silverstone model ridden by Gordon Keith, who won the 1964 Manx Grand Prix, setting fastest lap along the way.

In 1963 Greeves were asked to produce the bikes for the British team in the International Six Days Trial, replacing the four-stroke vertical twin machines which the team had used until then. Although these ISDT bikes used Villiers cranks, the bottom end was built by the Alpha company and they also contained large numbers of parts, including the barrels and heads, fabricated in Greeves' own factory. The company had of course embraced the technology of fibreglass moulding in the production of the Invacar and so were well able to produce lightweight fuel tanks, seats and mudguards for their bikes.

The new engine went into production in the 250cc Greeves Challenger of 1964 and a 360cc version appeared in 1967. Road-going machines were produced under the names Fleetmaster, Sportsman and Sports Twin; the Sports Twin being so well regarded in terms of both performance and reliability that it was adopted by many police forces.

However, the days of off-road dominance could not last forever. New challenges were on the horizon with fast, agile bikes from Spain and later Japan, enticing the top riders. Even Sammy Miller switched from Ariel to Bultaco in 1965. The last roadsters were made in 1968 but a new motocrosser with Greeves' own 360cc engine remained available until 1978, despite a disastrous fire at the works which effectively ended the Greeves story as far as volume production was concerned.

Of course there are still a large number of the tough little Greeves machines in existence, and they can still be seen in action in classic events. Ex-Trials rider Richard Deal began producing spares for Greeves machines in May 1999 and his company Greeves Motorsport has now begun production of what they call 'a new Trials bike for the 21st century'. The new 280cc Greeves has an aluminium frame produced from a solid billet and a modern engine manufactured using similar technology; it was publically launched at the Sammy Miller Museum in September 2010.

Bert Greeves was awarded the MBE in 1972 in recognition of his work for the disabled. He died on 15 July 1993.

Cotton

Frank Willoughby Cotton (known as 'F. W.' or 'Bill') competed in speed trials and motorcycle hillclimbs during 1912/13 and in 1914 he took over a small motorcycle manufacturer known as Sudbrook's from the original owner A. H. Camery. Production was halted by the First World War, but in 1918 he founded The Cotton Motorcycle Company in Gloucester. This company was run by its founder until his retirement in 1953.

As was virtually inevitable (and as with so many other motorcycle manufacturers of the day), F. W.'s thinking on motorcycle design began with bicycles, but he was one of the first to recognise that the standard diamond-shaped bicycle frame had serious limitations when an engine was added. He therefore devised a triangulated frame built using straight tubes. Also a lawyer, F. W. had the wisdom to patent his invention and all Cotton motorcycles were based on it until the Second World War. The first Cotton machine using this design appeared in 1920 and had a claimed top speed of 60 mph.

Privately owned Cottons quickly proved successful in speed trials and so, to promote his brand, F. W. decided to enter the Isle of Man TT in 1922 with a highly talented 18 year old, Stanley Woods, in the saddle, who was destined to become one of motorcycle racing's greats. On this first occasion, Woods and the Cotton finished fifth, but the following year he scored the first of his ten TT wins. Although competing in the Junior (350cc) race, Woods' time would also have been good enough to win the Senior.

This picture, taken at Kelly's Garage, Waterford, in 1930, clearly shows the Cotton triangulated frame which has managed to withstand a fairly heavy front end impact. (*Courtesy National Library of Ireland*)

Further TT success quickly followed, including a clean sweep of first, second and third in the 1926 Lightweight race – these bikes earned the nickname 'the Bobbins'. The Cotton was shown to be an exceptional machine with excellent handling and the order books were soon full, with production reaching 1,000 bikes per year. The company expanded its admittedly small workforce, and moved to new premises at the Vulcan Works in Quay Street, Gloucester. Local residents soon became accustomed to the sight of Cotton motorcycles being pushed to the town's two railway stations on their way to customers at home and abroad.

F. W. is known to have ordered a luxury car (a Sizaire-Berwick 25/50) at the 1923 Olympia Show; it is surely more than probable that this alone directly reflected the importance of that first TT win in terms of publicity and the prosperity of the firm. Then came the Depression years, but Cotton, still with a fairly small workforce and with a good range of models using engines from different sources, and enjoying a high reputation, were able to survive. In 1930 the engine choice comprised 250cc, 300cc, 350cc and 500cc engines, of two-stroke, four-stroke side-valve and four-stroke overhead-valve configurations made by Villiers, Blackburne and JAP. Since all the bikes shared similar straight-tube triangulated frames, excessive manufacturing complexity was avoided.

Throughout the 1930s the model range continued to change, often in direct response to the changing business environment. For example, in 1931 production of the Blackburne side-valve engines ceased, so Cotton bought in Rudge Python and Sturmey-Archer engines to replace them. By 1934 the range extended to nineteen models. The one thing which did not change to keep pace was of course the patented frame, and by the end of the 1930s this was no longer cutting edge in its performance. Solid frames were beginning to be replaced by various types of rear suspension.

One of the last of the pretty little Cotton 250cc race bikes. This one dates from 1980 and is fitted with the Rotax engine.

The Second World War provided light engineering work for the Cotton factory and after this they did not return to the motorcycle market until 1953, when Frank Cotton decided to retire. At this time the business was taken over by Elizabeth Cotton and reconstituted under the name E. Cotton (Motorcycles) Ltd, but managed by Pat Onions and Monty Denley.

The first machine produced by the Vulcan Works in this 'second era' was, appropriately enough, the Vulcan. This had a duplex frame, telescopic forks and a swinging arm rear and was given added sophistication for its day by the addition of rectified lighting, an electric horn and a dual seat. The brakes were also quite large and powerful. The Vulcan was powered by a Villiers 8E 197cc two-stroke engine and had a three-speed gearbox. Only the frame was actually made by Cotton and, unfortunately, a large part of the factory was occupied by the Ministry of Supply at this time. They didn't move out until 1960.

It has to be said that, although the original triangulated frame was clearly obsolete and had to be replaced, it had always been distinctive. A Cotton could be recognised and associated with the marque's racing heritage. The postwar Vulcan and its successors had lost this advantage and looked much like other Villiers-powered bikes of the period.

After the Vulcan there were several other models in the next few years; the Herald, Messenger, Double Gloucester (this was a sports twin), Continental, Corsair and Conquest were almost all Villiers powered, although the Cotanza was fitted with the less well known (but still British-made) Anzani for a short period in 1956/7. This later dependence on a single engine manufacturer, at odds with the pre-war practice, was ultimately to be the company's downfall.

Cotton moved back into the competition field in the postwar era, and by the time the entire factory floor was once again available to the workforce, they were producing a range of roadsters, trials and scrambler models. In 1961 a works scrambling team was established with Bryan Goss and John Draper as the riders, while from 1962 the 247cc Villiers Starmaker engine enabled the Cotton Telstar to make an impact in road racing.

In 1964 top race rider Derek Minter became Cotton's technical adviser and machines ridden by Minter, Bill Ivy and others won races on just about every British mainland circuit, with the result that production swung away from road models and was concentrated entirely on competition (race and scramble) bikes. Then, in 1966, Villiers were taken over by Manganese Bronze Holdings and, together with the failing AMC, were reformed as Norton-Villiers. At this point Villiers ceased supplying engines to outside companies and Villiers engine production moved to Madras, India. An Italian Minarelli engine was fitted to the Cotton Cavalier trials bikes, but only small numbers were produced.

In the 1970s the factory moved premises several times in and around Gloucester, before finally moving to Bolton in 1978. Here they produced a 250cc racing machine fitted with an Austrian Rotax engine, but in the end the financial difficulties became too great and Cotton closed down in 1980.

Douglas

William and Edward Douglas founded the Douglas Engineering Company in Bristol in 1882. Originally blacksmiths, they progressed to foundry work and then bought a failing motorcycle company, Light Motors Ltd, along with its design for a 200cc flat twin machine known as the 'Fair'.

The first bike to carry Douglas brothers' name went on sale in 1907 and within five years they were producing the technically interesting Model N. This featured a 350cc horizontally opposed twin engine with the cylinders facing fore and aft and the crankshaft across the frame. Most manufacturers of such bikes since have gone for the opposite arrangement, but this introduces a torque reaction which affects the handling. The Douglas was free of such problems and was successful in competition, with Tom Sheard using one to win the 1923 Senior TT. Alec Bennett won the Welsh TT in the same year and Freddie Dixon's leaning outfit triumphed in the first ever Manx sidecar race.

The engine crank drove a secondary shaft by chain and this then drove the rear wheel by belt running on the left side. The secondary shaft was equipped with pedals for starting the engine and these were also connected by chain to the right side of the rear wheel. In order to avoid the pedals spinning continuously the rear wheel was fitted with a freewheel mechanism on the pedal side. Electric lighting was added in 1915 and the machines were found to be ideal for military use. During the First World

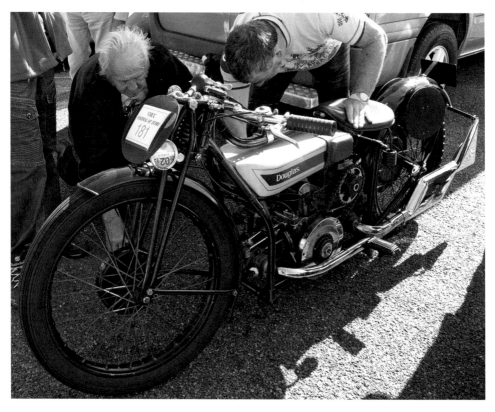

Above and below: The Douglas horizontally opposed engine which brought the company so much success. This bike dates from the mid-1920s.

War, Douglas were one of the largest suppliers of motorcycles. They are frequently reported to have supplied as many as 70,000 bikes to the Allied Forces.

The army, navy and the Royal Flying Corps (precursor of the RAF) all used two-wheeled vehicles, in part because of their off-road capabilities, which were important when roads were poor, damaged or simply blocked by other transport. Bikes were used by the Army Service Corps, the Royal Engineers and the Royal Artillery, and of course by despatch riders, who were vital to maintain communication links.

In the 1920s Douglas pioneered the use of disc brakes on motorcycles, although these were not their own invention, having been patented by Frederick Lanchester in 1902.

The quality of the firm's products was confirmed when they gained Royal Warrants as suppliers of motorcycles to two of the sons of King George V – Prince Albert (later King George VI, and the subject of the film *The King's Speech*) and Prince Henry, Duke of Gloucester. The older Prince, Albert, had seen action and been mentioned in despatches at Jutland during the recent war.

Douglas enjoyed major success in Dirt Track and Speedway racing in the late 1920s and early '30s with their DT5/6 and SW5/6 models. The '5' models were 500cc and the '6' denotes 600cc. These had hemispherical heads and short rigid cranks; around the turn of the decade they were particularly dominant on the dirt. In 1929 sales of Dirt Track motorcycles peaked at 1,200 units.

Unfortunately for Douglas, their extensive range proved to include too many expensive machines when the Depression hit in the 1930s, and they were among the motorcycle makers most severely affected. They were forced to call in the receivers in

Douglas machines gathered on the beach at Gallipoli in 1915. (*Photographer unknown*)

F. T. Hatton (Douglas) who made fastest time of the day.

Left: The happy Douglas-mounted winner of a 1920s time trial. (*Courtesy of Grace's Guide*)

Below: The 348cc Dragonfly was occasionally finished in black but this example may well be a repaint from the original cream.

1934 and their story would have ended at that point had not William Douglas poured his personal wealth into a rescue, which paralleled that launched by Jack Sangster at Ariel.

William Douglas had had a son, William Wilson Douglas, who was in control of the company from 1920, but he is known to have died in 1923 at the age of only 42 and so it seems that the William who saved the company must have been the original founding partner. He would by then have been quite an elderly man, but not necessarily older than John Marston when he made his first Sunbeam motorcycle.

Convinced of the need for an exciting new model to stimulate sales, the management charged the experimental department with its rapid development. The result was the Douglas Endeavour, which was, remarkably, ready to be introduced to the public at the Olympia Show which opened on 11 October 1934.

The four-speed Unit Construction 494cc machine departed from Douglas tradition in that its side-valve flat twin engine was mounted with its cylinders across the frame. It also featured shaft drive, which was the 'new thing' in the 1930s, but retained a hand-operated gearbox due to problems of accessibility for a foot change. The press received the bike warmly and parts for an initial run of 200 machines were made. Enthusiastic Douglas advertising described the Endeavour as

> The motorcycle of the age, a masterpiece on two wheels, car practice employed throughout, silent, safe, light, luxurious. The last word in engineering practice and design.

But such a bike was inevitably expensive. Its price tag of £72 10s put it in direct competition with the highly popular Rudge Ulster and consequently sales of the Endeavour were slow. It is likely that only about fifty of the original 200 were actually assembled and sold.

Douglas were sadly soon in trouble again, and were taken over by Aero Engines Ltd in 1935, and motorcycle production was reduced considerably. Remnant stock of Endeavour parts was discounted and sold off through a London dealer, though presumably some additional complete machines were eventually assembled by this route.

The Endeavour engine was shared with another new model, the Blue Chief, although in this bike its cylinders faced fore and aft in the traditional Douglas layout. The engine, which had a bore and stroke of 68 mm x 68 mm was genuinely quite advanced in design, having alloy cylinder liners and heads. The early Blue Chiefs, ordered by the War Office, seem to have had three-speed gearboxes, but the version offered to the public gained a fourth gear.

The last Douglas motorcycle was the 348cc Dragonfly of 1955 which, though heavy and consequently underpowered, did find favour with a section of the motorcycle buying public on its introduction at Earl's Court. Sadly Douglas were not able to meet this demand promptly, and it was some months before volume production could start. In the end only about 1,500 were made, and the last few were sold at discount in a manner reminiscent of the ill-fated Endeavour. Production finally ceased in 1957, although Douglas did import and assemble Vespa scooters and Gilera motorcycles until the 1960s.

Duzmo – 'Does More' (miles per hour)

John Wallace was born in 1896 and attended the Aske's Boys School, South London. He was determined to become an engineer, but this was not on the curriculum and his father wanted him to join the family clothing firm. Young John was not to be denied, however, and after a visit to a motorcycle exhibition at the age of 15, he decided not to buy a motorcycle but to build one.

He managed to buy a set of unmachined engine castings for £2 10s (£2.50) and set up a workshop in a garden shed. Unsurprisingly this enthusiastic but untutored project proved to be beyond him and beyond his tooling too, but undeterred, he bought a frame and wheels from a cycle maker and a second-hand engine, and not only produced his first motorbike but sold it too!

On leaving school, Wallace managed to overrule his father and get himself into an apprenticeship with the Collier Brothers of Matchless fame, but there was an accident of some sort at the factory and when Wallace senior heard about it he insisted that enough was enough and put a premature end to his son's fledgling employment.

All was not lost though; he bought two Rudge bikes for John and his brother, and John promptly joined the British Motor Cycle Racing Club and began a racing career at Brooklands. Unfortunately 'things did not go well' and John's Rudge was soon no more.

He must have been doing something right though, as in 1913, while still only 17 years old, he managed to get accepted as a test rider for the JAP company; a job which required some riding at Brooklands. Then they found out how old he was and he was immediately unemployed again. Even now all was not lost as he spent the next year filling in the important gap in his education by studying engineering and training to become a draughtsman.

During his brief career as a racer/test rider, he had met and befriended no less a person than Bert LeVack, himself a JAP tester at the time, and when the First World War arrived, both Wallace and LeVack took their engineering abilities to the Scottish aircraft firm of Arrol-Johnston. This was again a short-lived position, and Wallace moved on to a job with the design team at Westland Aircraft Company (Petters) Ltd until the end of the war.

Now Wallace demonstrated the sort of entrepreneurial spirit which a young lad without relevant qualifications certainly needs. He realised that, following the war, there would be many engineering companies whose order books, until recently filled by war work, would now be empty. He designed a motorcycle engine and advertised it, not in the motorcycling press, such as it may have been at that difficult time, but in *The Aeroplane*, offering it to any firm wishing to diversify, now that wartime contracts had ended.

The design was good and the Portable Tool and Engineering Company of Enfield, Middlesex, not only applied for the rights to produce the engine with a view to selling it to other motorcycle manufacturers, but also took on the young man Wallace as their Chief Designer. He may of course have been head of a one-man department, but it was the sort of opportunity he had wanted, and by September 1919 the engine was ready for trials.

At this point, Wallace's friendship with Bert LeVack was renewed. Conveniently LeVack, trying to make a living as a garage proprietor, had found that life as a self-employed businessman didn't suit him, and he accepted a job with Portable Tool at an affordable rate of pay.

Not only did LeVack have wartime experience of assembling and testing engines which would complement Wallace's design experience, but he was simply very good at the 'down to earth' aspects of making ill-fitting components fit and work. He was a good mechanic – and time would prove that he was a superb test rider and an advertising 'gift' into the bargain.

It was Bert who actually built the first prototype engine, and after building a second, he fitted it into a complete motorcycle, which he then used in both competitions and in public and trade demonstrations. The machine was initially called the 'Ace', then the 'Buzmo', until the name Duzmo was arrived at and retained. There is a suggestion that it was meant to mean 'does more' (mph?) and this at least seems as reasonable as any other explanation.

It is hardly surprising that a good machine – which the Duzmo surely was – ridden by a rider of Bert LeVack's calibre attracted attention, and that this resulted in orders. In addition, Wallace and LeVack had produced a second prototype bike in 1920 with a 50-degree V-twin engine, consisting essentially of a pair of the Duzmo 496cc singles mated onto a new bottom end. This machine was entered in the Brooklands 200-mile sidecar race that year. So many orders flooded in that the small company could not possibly build enough motorcycles to meet the demand.

The only way forward was to float the company on the Stock Market, issuing shares so that investment would be available to fund the necessary expansion of manufacturing capacity. Unfortunately, all of this rapid growth seems to have been too much for the directors of the Portable Tool Company. They were unwilling to adopt the recommended course of action and decided instead to wind up the company; a true case of a business becoming a victim of its own success. One can only imagine how the entrepreneur John Wallace must have felt about such a decision. Bert LeVack received an offer from Hendee, the builders of Indian motorcycles, and he too was lost to the cause.

Once again, however, all was not lost. One of the directors of the Portable Tool Company was prepared to demonstrate faith in Wallace by backing him personally. He lent the money Wallace would need to take over the company himself, with the loan to be repaid from future profits. Duzmo motorcycles could continue in production, but now they were to be produced by John Wallace's own company, with engine building contracted out to the Advance Motor Manufacturing Company of Nottingham.

What of the machine itself? It was an uncompromising sports machine, designed from the start by Wallace with definite racing intent. The Duzmo in its 1920 production form was a belt-drive 496cc single with exposed overhead valves and an aluminium piston. The engine was pressure lubricated and was really quite advanced for the day.

For 1921 there were a few design modifications to the single-cylinder machine, and also a production version of the V-twin, which had a Sturmey-Archer gearbox and all chain drive as standard, but perhaps rather oddly, there was also a single-speed belt drive option available. Duzmo entered bikes in the Isle of Man TT in both 1920 and 1921, but without success as there were problems with reliability.

Without Bert LeVack, the Duzmo name began to fade from the limelight fairly quickly, and for 1923 the V-twin was dropped. A revised 496cc bike arrived for the 1924 season with a new frame providing for a sloping engine and a 'banana' tank. These two features together meant that the seating position could be lowered. The machine now had a three-speed Sturmey-Archer gearbox and all chain drive, as on the earlier V-twin but now the orders simply weren't there and John Wallace was forced into liquidation, selling the remainder of his business to D. J. Shepherd and Co. in February 1924. Shepherds attempted to distribute Duzmo motorcycles for a time, but there seems to be no definite evidence of any actual sales.

It is clear that John Wallace was a determined young man and a talented designer who perhaps deserved greater success than he ever achieved. However, it appears that after the final 1924 debacle, he accepted that he had given the motorcycle industry enough of his time and energy for he never worked in it again. He did continue to design engines, including a never-built single-cylinder gear-driven overhead cam unit and a straight eight two-stroke. Wallace also wrote about issues such as 'wheel wobble', but returned to aircraft for his employment, designing a seven-cylinder radial aero engine and working as a design draughtsman at D. Napier and Sons, until his retirement in the 1960s, by which time he was chief test plant engineer, and Napiers had been taken over by English Electric. Rolls Royce took over the aero engine side of the business in 1961, and it is possible that this would have coincided with John Wallace's retirement. He died in 1983 at the age of 87.

DOT – 'Devoid Of Trouble'

The DOT was made in Salford, now officially part of Greater Manchester, but in reality and history a city in its own right, even though the centres are a mere half mile apart. This machine was made to a higher standard of both specification and finish than many of its contemporaries, with its neat 'crimped' tank and adjustable dampers.

The early girder-type fork was actually a remarkably long-lived design. Even though manufacturers such as Scott had begun to experiment with telescopic arrangements between the wars and Matchless were using hydraulically damped telescopic forks in the 1930s, there were those (Phil Vincent chief among them) who felt that the inherent lack of stiffness of a telescopic fork would always render them inadequate – at least for heavy and powerful motorcycles.

However, the DOT B1 in the pictures deserves mention here for more than just its front forks. The Bradshaw oil-cooled engine was revolutionary in a day when 'total

The DOT B1 friction damper.

The Salford-made DOT B1 Bradshaw.

The Bradshaw oil-cooled engine (with evidence of a leak?) as fitted to the DOT B1. Only the cylinder head requires cooling fins.

loss' lubrication systems and air cooling were the norm. The Bradshaw contained its oil in a sump, and what is more, oil from the sump served the secondary purpose of cooling the cylinder wall and main bearings. The engine gained the unflattering (and almost certainly unfair) nickname of 'oil boiler', but was used in a number of different makes of motorcycle. Note the smooth cylinder walls. Only the head carries cooling fins.

Granville Bradshaw was in fact an imaginative and experimental engineer and it is perhaps for this reason that his failures are sometimes remembered more than his achievements. His toroidal engine occupied a great deal of his time but never made it to production, while the ABC Dragonfly radial design was once described as the engine which would have lost Britain the Great War had it continued another year. However, it is likely that this remark was actually a criticism of the First World War Air Board, who were planning to put an untried engine into large-scale production, rather than a swipe at its design.

Bradshaw was responsible in the 1920s for the ABC 400cc motorcycle with its then revolutionary horizontally opposed twin-cylinder engine. Such engines have been used extensively since, most notably in BMW machines.

Rex-Acme

Rex Motorcycles was founded in Birmingham in 1899 by William and Harold Williamson and retained its name after a merger with Allard bicycles of Coventry in 1902. Motorcycle manufacture began in 1904 and Billy Heaton finished second in the twin-cylinder class at the inaugural TT of 1907, riding a bike equipped with Rex's own recently pioneered sprung fork. The 1908 model was the first to use an angled-down top tube to lower the riding position.

In 1911 the Williamsons were sacked from the business and under a new a managing director, George Hemingway, they went on to design and build their own engines, although a range of bikes was produced for Premier using JAP engines. At this stage they were responsible for a number of innovations, including the use of rotary valves as they experimented with 350cc two-strokes and shaft-drive V-twins. The company continued to manufacture engines into the 1920s, after which they used proprietary units.

Wal Handley turning in at Creg-Ny-Baa corner on his 350cc Rex-Acme during the 1926 Isle of Man Junior TT. (*Photographer unknown*)

Coventry Acme were bought out in 1919, and in 1921, after the ranges had been rationalised, the name was changed to Rex-Acme. At its most successful, the Rex-Acme catalogue included fifteen models from 172cc to 746cc.

The great rider Walter Handley, then a rising young star, brought them fame through his racing exploits, winning the 1923 Ulster Grand Prix and scoring TT wins in 1925 (both the Ultra Lightweight and Junior) and 1927. He also set numerous speed records at Brooklands and actually became a director of the company for a time.

Though he left in 1928 to ride for other firms, including the Swiss Motosacoche who were making big strides at the time and had Bert LeVack working for them, Handley did not sever all ties with Rex-Acme. He actually rode for them as late as the 1930 Lightweight TT on a Blackburne-powered 173cc single, though he did not finish on this occasion.

Handley was not the only well-known rider of the day to race on Rex-Acme machines. Others included Arthur Taylor, Felice Bonetto, and Otto Cecconi, but without Handley the name rapidly faded. The company soon became a victim of the Depression, but the range was actually increased in an unsuccessful attempt to stimulate sales. There was even a Speedway bike on offer, but the financial situation continued to worsen and the business was sold to sidecar maker Mills-Fulford in 1932. Production of motorcycles ceased the following year.

James

In the postwar years of the 1940s and 1950s, money was tight; 'pool' petrol was of low quality and low octane rating (around 77) and consequently engines ran at low compression ratios and needed de-coking regularly. In this climate, cars were comparatively few and motorcycles numerous. Fitted with sidecars they were family transport, and without they got people to work.

Powerful bikes were suited to sidecar use, but something smaller was better for commuting. Two-stroke engines offered simplicity, which made them cheap to make and easy for the owner to maintain, and so most manufacturers included small two-stroke bikes in their range.

The James company was one such manufacturer. The firm produced its first motorbike in 1902 and became part of the AMC group in 1951. The model shown is a Colonel K12 of 1955, powered by a two-stroke Villiers engine of 225cc and finished in the typical James maroon. Note the neat cast metal housing for the carburettor

The 225cc engine size enabled it to fit into a lower tax band and possibly also made it cheaper to insure than a conventional 'just below 250cc' machine. The bike has a low seat, and it has been suggested to me that this served to make it more appealing to older riders. However, most bikes from this period were low-slung by modern standards, and this is surely a reflection of the greater lean angles possible when cornering on modern tyres.

Practicality with elegance; the 225cc James Colonel.

Zenith

Zenith was another of the really early ones. Founded in Finsbury Park in 1904, they initially used a variety of engines including Villiers and Precision. The first machine was something of a novelty, and originally appeared at the Crystal Palace Show in 1905 under the name of the Tooley Bi-Car, after its inventor. However, just a few months later, an improved version was produced with the name changed to Zenith. This machine was advertised as 'the finest mechanical frame yet designed' with the prediction that it would 'absolutely revolutionise the construction of motor bicycles'. Powered by a 3-hp Fafnir engine, the Bi-Car had a frame that deviated completely from those based on pedal bicycles. A single horizontal tube ran from one end of the rear wheel spindle right past the end of the front wheel spindle, around the front of the machine and back to the opposite end of the rear spindle. A second 'frame', suspended below the first to eliminate vibration, carried the weight of the rider, and the engine and the machine used hub-centred steering so that the handlebar was placed a long way behind the conventional position. Later models gained a 5-hp engine and two speeds, but in the end, the Bi-Car did not revolutionise anything. It did, however, illustrate this maker's willingness to think 'outside the box' – an appropriate enough

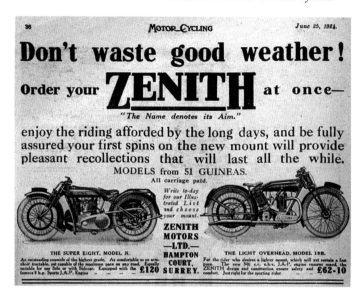

Advert for Zenith Motors. (*Courtesy of Grace's Guide*)

trait when dealing with such a young technology.

By 1907 they introduced the Zenette, designed by the firm's newly appointed chief engineer Frederic 'Freddy' Barnes. This was a 500cc machine with a more recognisable frame, but nevertheless still innovative in design. A pair of straight tubes ran down from the head bearing to the crankcase and could be seen as having quite a 'modern' look. The steering was by an ordinary girder fork.

Although they quickly seem to have realised the practical necessity of building frames based on reasonably conventional ideas, Zenith remained forward-thinking, producing the 'Gradua' variable gearing in 1908/9. Previously, since most bikes of the period were driven by leather belts, changing gear was generally only possible if yours was fitted with a second pair of pulleys so that you could hop off and physically move the belt every time you came to a hill. Of course this would normally mean that the belt run changed length and so you also needed to carry a spare belt of a different length – possibly in addition to the spare you carried anyway in case of breakage.

The Zenith Gradua system, developed by Freddy Barnes, used a pulley (on some models this was itself driven from the engine by a short primary chain) whose side walls could be moved closer together when required. This pushed the pulley higher and so, in effect, the pulley increased in diameter. This alteration was achieved by winding a handle to the left of the petrol tank so it could be done while the bike was moving.

Of course, if that had been the whole story then the belt tension, critical if the drive was to be maintained, would either increase to breaking point as the pulley walls were moved together, or decrease to the point at which the belt would slip hopelessly as the walls moved apart.

Barnes came up with an automatically adjusting tensioner. The rear wheel spindle was mounted in slots which allowed it to move backwards to increase tension and forward to reduce it. This action was produced by a pair of bevel gears on the bottom of the gear changing shaft which the rider was turning. The mechanism for the left side was connected to the right by a short chain. The variation in gearing was fairly limited but the system worked. It was essentially similar to the 'Multigear' which Zenith's competitors Rudge introduced in the same year, although the Rudge system was more sophisticated and gave a greater range of adjustment. Rudge were only able to produce the Multigear due to their long experience of manufacturing extremely accurate bicycle wheels, since it required two separate 'wheels', each with forty spokes, to run concentrically on the rear wheel spindle.

But the Zenith Gradua clearly outperformed contemporary single-speed machines of the same power, and many clubs banned it from competing in their events as it was judged to have an unfair advantage. As Alfred Scott would do later when his two-strokes were considered unfairly powerful, Zenith attempted to turn the ban to their advantage in selling their motorcycles; they simply added the word 'Barred' in bold red lettering to the company logo. How significant this may have been in sales terms is difficult to say.

Both the Zenith and Rudge transmission systems remained in production until the mid-1920s, by which time the countershaft gearboxes and chain drives of manufacturers such as Scott, Royal Enfield, Sturmey-Archer and others had finally asserted themselves.

It is often forgotten that Zenith had a great deal of success in competitive events. They were, for a time, among the fastest motorcycles made anywhere and held a number of speed records at Brooklands in the 1920s. If you wanted to win a Gold Star for a lap at 100 mph or above, and you were one of the majority who couldn't afford a Brough Superior, a Zenith was a 'best buy'. The company actually moved to Weybridge, just down the road from Brooklands when the track opened in 1909, in order to have the facility on hand, and Freddy Barnes was himself a frequent race winner, mixing it enthusiastically with his customers in the years leading up to the First World War.

Zenith took part in military trials in the immediate pre-war period and did well, but for some reason they do not seem to have been awarded contracts to supply military motorcycles. This work went to the Douglas factory instead. The Zenith works in Weybridge did apparently do some form of war work but records are scarce and it is not even clear whether Barnes remained in Britain or served abroad.

There was no racing at Brooklands until 1920 due to bomb damage sustained, thanks to the tempting presence of the Vickers aircraft factory, but when competition resumed, Zenith were there, with Freddy Barnes now on hand to support rather than to race.

The very first official 100 mph run on a motorcycle in Britain was achieved at Brooklands in 1921 by Douglas Davidson on a Harley-Davidson (thereby winning the 'Godfrey Cup' which had been offered for this), but Bert LeVack, working for J. A. Prestwich as a test rider, not only repeated the feat the following year on a 998cc Zenith-JAP, but also set the first 100 mph-plus motorcycle lap of the Brooklands outer circuit.

In the 1930s, Zenith were one of the many companies forced into bankruptcy by the Depression, and although the company was rescued and enabled to return to motorcycle production, Freddy Barnes and Brooklands played little part in the revamped company's career.

Unfortunately, innovative or not, Zenith never took the big step into engine manufacture. They always relied on buying them in; through much of their history they relied primarily on JAP motors of all sizes up to 1,100cc. There was a 1922 horizontally opposed twin, powered by an oil-cooled Bradshaw engine, but this was an exception.

When the Second World War broke out, Zenith actually had a large stock of 750cc V-twin JAP engines, and although they could not produce motorcycles during the war years, they were able to begin again immediately afterwards; but only until they ran out of engines. This was a period in which proprietary engines were scarce and Zenith were forced to cease production permanently in 1950.

Scott

As has been noted, front suspension design tended to move on much more rapidly than rear. The telescopic fork actually made its first tentative appearance in the very early days of motorcycling. Alfred Scott, a brilliant and innovative engineer from Bradford, designed a twin-cylinder two-stroke motorcycle with a semi-telescopic fork which was built for him by the Jowett company of Bradford, now chiefly remembered for cars such as the 'Jupiter' model, one of which was later bought second-hand by a young Vincent apprentice named John Surtees. He has since spoken very highly of it.

In Britain at least, the modern telescopic fork with internal hydraulic damping had to wait until the 1930s, when Matchless fitted their machines with the 'teledraulic' fork, which was itself based on a BMW design.

The Scott of 1908 was well ahead of its time, not only having the telescopic forks,

This lady is riding a 1911 Scott. The basic design is already fairly well established although the small cylindrical fuel tank is hidden by her skirt! (*Courtesy of Grace's Guide*)

Above, below and next page: Richard Blackburn's Scott was originally intended to race in the 1928 Sidecar TT. Now in road trim, it provides a great advertisement for his skills as a restorer.

Above and right: Barry Lain's
1929 Flying Squirrel is a
partially restored (so far at least)
'barn find'. The orange barrels
may be the original colour?
The engine is another that has
benefited from time spent in
Richard Blackburn's workshop.

Sadly, even an innovative company can become stale. This 1947 machine shows far too little evidence of further progress.

but also being equipped with a kickstarter at a time when riders of other makes had to be able to bump start them; no easy job as anyone who has done it will know. The Scott was also not fitted with pedals. Its designer was presumably confident they would simply not be needed. Possibly the most significant feature of all was the use of a water-cooled cylinder head, Scott having taken out the relevant patents. It took a little longer (though only until 1914) for the cylinders also to be contained within a full water jacket. It is interesting to note though (and remarkable) that the 1894 Hildebrand and Wolfmuller machine described in Chapter One did actually have a fully water-cooled engine.

By 1910, Scott even had a two-speed drive operated by a foot pedal. Scott and his machine were successful in hillclimb events; so much so that moves were made to have it banned. It was claimed that the two-stroke engine had an unfair advantage since it fired twice as often as the more conventional four-strokes. The machine was not banned, but a handicap was applied. The Scott bikes were deemed to have 1.32 times their actual capacity for competition purposes. Of course, Scott, a businessman as well as an engineer, made great use of this in his future advertising! 'The machine everyone else is afraid of…'

Demand for Scott motorcycles now required him to set up his own factory in Saltaire, a Yorkshire village on the River Aire, founded by the enlightened Victorian mill owner Sir Titus Salt.

Scott's machines were highly successful in the Isle of Man, scoring TT wins in 1912 and 1913, and setting record lap speeds in several other years. C. P. 'Clarry' Wood also won the 1922 Welsh TT on Pendine Sands, riding the newly introduced and ferociously loud Scott Squirrel. This engine was said to have drawn complaints from the monks on Caldey Island across the bay from the Pendine race!

Richard Blackburn's machine seen on pages 91 and 92 is one of eight built by the factory for the Isle of Man TT in 1928. This was the number two machine for the sidecar event, but as the race was cancelled it was not raced that year. It was then registered for road use and used for practise and testing.

However, the new engine developed for the 1930 TT was not a success (I have heard it described more colourfully as a disaster) and the 1928 bikes, including this one, were eventually raced. One of the riders, Bill Kitchen (later to become a prominent speedway rider), is recorded as having a minor 'off' at Creg-ny-Baa, a fast right-hand bend at the end of the mountain section of the course, and the Scott entries did not figure among the leading finishers.

The bike was then recorded as 'scrapped' by the factory, but in fact it was raced for more than 20 years by Cliff Kingham. Restored to Concours condition in 2011, it is now back on the road.

New Imperial

New Imperial were another of the bicycle companies from the late Victorian era whose move into motorcycle production more or less coincided with the queen's death. In their case, it was quite a close coincidence as the first New Imperial motorcycle was produced in 1901.

The company was founded in Birmingham by Norman Downes and initially made bicycle fittings. Complete bicycles were in production by the end of the nineteenth century, possibly after Downes bought out the failing Hearl and Tonks bicycle works. Downes moved to new premises and renamed the company New Imperial Cycles, but the dates of these moves are not known. There are records of the formation of a limited company of that name as late as 1908, but bicycles and indeed motorcycles were in production, apparently under the New Imperial name, much earlier.

The first machine New Imperial motorcycle was actually just one of the firm's bicycles with an engine added. Admittedly this was in the days before designers had made up their minds that the engine was best positioned low down, centrally in the frame, and that it should drive the rear wheel, pretty much just replacing the cyclist's pedals. The New Imperial simply carried its engine in the easiest place to strap it on; above the front wheel, in front of the handlebars. From this position its leather belt transmission was of course restricted to driving the front wheel.

Left: This 500cc New Imperial Clubman dates from the late 1930s. The tank decal appears to be on the wrong side – the lion normally faced forwards.

Below: The Matchless G9 was the twin brother of the AJS Model 20.

This machine was not one that impressed the public and it did not sell. In fact, it is said that not even one was sold, and that the engines were taken back to the works and later used to power machinery. New Imperial retreated back into the safety of bicycle manufacture for the time being.

They tried again in 1910 and this time they did it properly, designing a conventional motorcycle frame to fit a 293cc JAP engine. By 1912/13 there were three models in the New Imperial range: a 500cc JAP-engined bike, an 8-hp V-twin machine intended specifically for sidecar use, and in 1914 the 'Light Tourist'. This bike would become famous as its light, strong frame enabled its little engine to outperform many 500cc bikes of the day. The New Imperial Light Tourist was a bike the public could take to and this time sales were brisk. The bike remained in production into the 1920s and the company was on its way.

Three of the 500cc machines were entered in the Isle of Man TT for 1913, since this event was already a 'must do' for any motorcycle manufacturer serious about selling bikes in large numbers. On this occasion though, success proved elusive as all three bikes retired with mechanical problems. There were only twenty-four finishers in all from eighty-seven starters, which illustrates just what a tough test the recently introduced Mountain Circuit was for these early bikes.

Following the First World War, sales continued to be strong and prospects were bright. Even racing victory now came their way as Doug Prentice rode a New Imperial to win the 250cc Lightweight class at the 1921 TT. Technically this was not a 'TT win' as the race was run as a class within the Junior TT until 1922, but it was a sales booster just the same. It was to be followed by five more 'full' TT wins for the company, all but one in the Lightweight category.

Bert LeVack joined the company as a rider for a short while, coming close to winning the Lightweight race in 1923. The bike stopped, most likely due to running out of fuel, half a mile from the finish, and Bert pushed it home to take second place. Many a rider has had this experience, and as the last half mile is uphill, they tend to find it a test of their determination.

In the following year, 1924, the Twemlow brothers, Ken and Eddie, achieved a double success, winning both the Lightweight and Junior races for New Imperial, boosting sales further.

By the mid-1920s New Imperial production was running at around 300 motorcycles per month, and prosperity continued until the end of the decade. In 1926 they began to manufacture their own engines for the first time, having always used JAP and Precision power until that point. JAP engines remained an optional fitment for a time, but were eventually dropped completely. In 1929 the company left their premises in Birmingham's gun quarter and moved into a new purpose-built factory on a 6-acre site at Hall Green. Then the Depression hit in the 1930s and manufacturers everywhere suffered. Many motorcycle makers went out of business quite quickly, but New Imperial managed to carry on.

In 1934 Ginger Woods, riding a New Imperial 500 cc V-twin, won the prestigious 'Motor Cycle' Trophy when he maintained a 102.2 mph average speed for one hour at Brooklands. This was the first time a 500cc multi-cylinder bike had exceeded 100 mph at the track.

Further TT success came the factory's way in 1936 when Bob Foster won the Lightweight TT on a sprung-frame, unit-construction New Imperial, the last British four-stroke to win this event. This bike was an example of genuinely innovative design and was arguably 20 years ahead of its time, but even this was not ultimately enough. The company's financial strength had been drained by trading in the near impossible circumstances of the Depression. Additionally, the company's founder Norman Downes had died in 1938, and the receivers were called in. New Imperial was advertised for sale on 18 November.

On 30 December Jack Sangster, of Ariel and Triumph, announced that he had bought the company and production resumed on 27 January 1939. In early February the faltering firm was again sold, this time to Solomon Joseph, owner of Clifford Covering and Motor Components, and production continued.

The Second World War began in September and almost immediately all New Imperial spare parts were sold to the Collier brothers of AMC. Now New Imperial Ltd officially changed their name to Clifford Aero & Auto Ltd, Aeronautical Engineers, and they switched production to aeronautical components for the war effort.

It was reported that the name New Imperial was sold to BSA by Jack Sangster at a later date, but it is of course possible that he retained this when he sold the factory and spares. Something similar happened with the JAP name as has been recorded elsewhere in this book. Suffice it to say that no more motorcycles were ever produced with the New Imperial 'Lion' logo on the petrol tank after 1939.

Omega

There was more than one company which made motorcycles under the name Omega, but the one which lasted longest was 'W. J. Green Ltd – Motor Engineers' of Coventry. James Green had worked for both Humber and William Hillman's Premier Company before the First World War, and set up his own business in 1918 when Premier closed down. His first models left the works in 1919 and were powered by Blackburne and Villiers engines, but he soon designed and produced his own 170cc and 348cc two-strokes. Other engines fitted to Omega machines included JAP, Bradshaw and Barr and Stroud. Green added sidecars to his range from 1920 and even built a three-wheeler car between 1925 and 1927.

An Omega owned by Welsh racer Billy Edwards is known to have raced at Pendine Sands in the 1920s and this bike still exists, but on the whole survivors are rare. Production ended in 1927.

OK-Supreme

OK and OK-Supreme machines were made in Birmingham from 1899 until 1939, with grass-track racing versions continuing to be available until 1946. The OK company was founded in 1882 by Major Ernest Humphries and Charles Dawes to manufacture bicycles. The Dawes name can of course still be seen on modern bicycle frames, but between 1899 and 1906 the partners experimented with powered machines, and by 1911 they were ready to begin manufacture of a motorcycle using the already well-established Precision engine. This was the year in which Precision are known to have provided the power for no less than ninety-six of the motorcycles exhibited at the Olympia Show.

The 1912 TT yielded a ninth place finish, but OK had to wait until 1928 for their first win when Frank Longman headed home the Lightweight race at an average speed of just less than 63 mph. Wal Handley had set the fastest lap in 1922 but the bike did not finish on that occasion.

Following the end of the First World War, OK produced their own 292cc two-stroke engine, but they also continued to use Blackburne, Bradshaw and JAP units. The race bikes in particular were JAP powered. Charles Dawes left to produce bicycles under his own name in 1926 and the OK company was renamed OK-Supreme shortly after.

In 1928 the HRD company failed and Humphries bought the factory and tooling, but sold-on the name and customer base to one Phil Vincent, who did rather well with it!

The 'Lighthouse' model, named for the inspection window in the cam tower, marked the end of the road for OK-Supreme in 1939, although as mentioned earlier, Humphries' son John continued to sell a 350cc JAP-engined grass-tracker until his death in 1946.

Grindlay-Peerless

Alfred Grindlay and Edward Peerless formed the Grindlay-Peerless company in Coventry in 1923 and initially built extremely high quality sidecars. It was natural that when they decided to produce a motorcycle it should also be a machine of distinction, and large enough to power a sidecar outfit. Hence they missed out the usual steps of building smaller bikes first. The external similarity between the early G-P and the Brough Superior is immediately obvious and probably the main reason the bikes tend to be less widely known is simply that few were made and consequently very few survive.

Nevertheless, in their day, they set records and achieved a great reputation. It could even be argued that the standard of finish surpassed the Brough, with monograms pressed into the exhausts, a beautifully shaped fuel tank shining with brightly coloured cadmium and nickel plating, and a luxurious leather covered saddle. However, it is not only the appearance of a Grindlay-Peerless which makes it significant. The engineering, particularly that of the early models, also demands attention.

These large, comfortable, touring motorcycles used a Barr and Stroud 999cc V-twin engine of unusual design. Although they were four-strokes, they displayed a 'clean' top end with none of the usual push-rods and rockers etc. to operate the valves. Nowadays the 'poppet' valve is so ubiquitous that earlier types have been largely forgotten, yet in the 1920s a number of makers of cars and aircraft used an alternative type since the early poppet valves had certain disadvantages. Poppets needed decoking regularly and only lasted about 20,000 miles (or the equivalent number of hours in aircraft applications) before a full regrinding job was called for. The alternative was the sleeve valve (*see Glossary*).

The Barr and Stroud engine was rugged and produced plenty of torque, combined with a spread of power throughout the rev range. This made it an excellent power unit for motorcycle use.

This 999cc model had a three-speed Sturmey-Archer gearbox and chain drive but was only produced for four years. It was one of the more expensive machines on the market, but at least one fine 1924 example still exists, on display in the Sammy Miller Motorcycle Museum in Hampshire. A 499cc sleeve-valve machine was also produced from 1925 onward and one of these can also be seen at the Miller museum.

The marque achieved major competitive success in the hands of C. W. G. 'Bill' Lacey. Lacey was a famed engine tuner, working particularly on Nortons, but was also one of the better race riders of the 1920s, making his first appearance at Brooklands in 1922 riding a Rudge Multi. His first win came in 1924 on a 350cc Cotton, and his machines quickly became noted for their superb preparation; by no means the norm at Brooklands! His motto was 'no finish, no win'.

Switching to a pair of 350cc and 500cc Grindlay-Peerless-JAPs, Lacey soon won the coveted Gold Star (awarded to a rider when he achieved his first 100 mph lap) and in 1928 he went on to become the first rider to average 100 mph for one hour on a machine of less than 500cc on British soil, covering 103 miles in the hour. G-P quickly responded to this by producing a replica machine – the Brooklands 'Hundred Model', although only five or six of these were ever made.

Although Bert Denly beat this at Montlhéry the following August, Lacey went to the same track and raised the mark to just over 105 miles. He eventually covered 111 miles in an hour on a Norton in 1931.

In the 1950s and '60s, Lacey was persuaded to prepare race engines for several riders including the up and coming Mike Hailwood, whose 1961 Senior TT win was achieved on a Lacey-tuned Norton. He learned to fly a microlight aircraft at the age of 85 and died in 1989 at the age of 88.

Grindlay-Peerless expanded their range over the years to include machines powered by a variety of engines, mainly from JAP and Rudge (whose factory was nearby), but there were a couple of two-stroke machines with 172cc, 196cc and 247cc Villiers motors too.

By 1933 the company's most prosperous years were behind them, and motorcycle production ceased in 1934, with the firm turning its attention to other products.

Excelsior

Excelsior are a company with a claim to being the first British motorcycle maker of all. The firm was founded under the name of Bayliss, Thomas and Company in 1874 (and indeed this date was the boast on the machines' tank badges) in Lower Ford

Street, Coventry, and made high-wheel bicycles – the type commonly known as penny farthings. They made their first powered machines in 1896, using Belgian Minerva engines among others.

The company name was changed to Excelsior Motor Company in 1910, but the name 'Bayliss-Thomas' was still to be seen on fuel tanks until at least 1927. Excelsior gained a major contract to supply the Russian government with a JAP-powered twin, but this deal was lost with the 1917 revolution. Excelsior were now in trouble, carrying a large quantity of unsold stock; as a result, after the First World War, the business was bought by R. Walker and Sons who had previously been one of its major suppliers. Production moved from Coventry to the Walkers' home town of Tyseley, Birmingham, and the Coventry factory was sold to the Francis-Barnett company.

Motorcycle production continued in this postwar period, and now the engines came from Blackburne, JAP and Villiers. However, there was a major change. In addition to the lightweight low-cost bikes, Excelsior introduced the much more expensive 'Manxman' model in three engine sizes – 250cc, 350cc and 500cc. These overhead-camshaft-engined motorcycles were designed by H. J. Hatch and Eric Walker (one of

Above left: Typical small two-stroke Villiers engine installed in an Excelsior machine.

Above and previous page right: The Excelsior Manxman is another machine which just looks 'right'.

proprietor Reginald Walker's sons) and were marketed both as sporty roadsters and out and out racers.

While not one of the 'great' race bikes, the Manxman certainly achieved enough to raise the status of the company in the public perception during the inter-war years. There were several second places in the Isle of Man and a win in the 1936 European Grand Prix in Germany.

As there were no engine building facilities at the Excelsior works until after the Second World War, the Manxman engines were built initially by the firm of Blackburnes in Farnham, and later by the Black Country founders, Beans Industries.

Chapter 6

Not Everyone Stopped Making Bicycles

Rudge

A merger of two bicycle manufacturers in 1894 led to the establishment of Rudge Whitworth Cycles. The company, based in Coventry (snappy advertising slogan 'Rudge it, do not trudge it' – yes, really!), began selling re-badged Werner motorcycles in 1909 and produced their own first motorcycle in 1911 using a 500cc single-cylinder inlet-over-exhaust (IOE) configuration.

For 1912 the company produced a highly innovative machine, the Rudge Multigear. This was an elegant masterpiece and relied heavily on the fact that Rudge, as a world-renowned bicycle maker, had developed the ability to manufacture spoked wheels to exacting standards.

At this time pioneer motorcyclists were well used to the smoothness and cheapness of leather belts to transfer drive from the engine to the rear wheel, but the problem of changing gear had yet to be solved. The belt normally had to be moved from one pulley to another of a different diameter and this meant fitting a different belt in order to compensate for the different length of the belt run. Not an ideal manoeuvre to carry out – twice – every time you came to a hill.

Zenith had come up with a partial answer in the same year by fitting an engine pulley with walls that could be squeezed together to cause the belt to ride up higher, effectively giving a larger diameter pulley. The change in belt tension was addressed by a bevel gear linked to the pulley mechanism, which was capable of moving the rear wheel forward or back by the required amount. However, this gave only a limited variation in gearing.

The Rudge solution used a *pair* of variable-groove-depth pulleys. The walls of the belt groove were again moved closer together to squeeze the belt higher and increase the effective diameter of the pulley. The gear lever at the side of the Rudge fuel tank, which adjusted the engine pulley walls inwards, also moved the rear wheel pulley walls outwards (or vice versa) simultaneously, thereby altering the ratio and maintaining a constant tension in the belt.

The rear wheel was effectively two separate wheels running concentrically. One carried the tyre and the inner wall of the pulley, the other carried the outer wall of

Advert for Rudge. (*Courtesy of Grace's Guide*)

the pulley. Each had forty spokes and the two sets of spokes were interwoven. As stated above it surely would have been well nigh impossible for any non-bicycle manufacturer to make such an arrangement work.

The complex-sounding system actually worked well and reliably, and provided not simply two ratios but, along with the at least equally complex Zenith Gradua system introduced in the same year, it made continuously variable transmissions a reality. Ratios available ranged between approximately 3½:1 and 7:1.

A Rudge Multi won the TT in 1914 and was the first single-cylinder machine to do so. The rider, 21-year-old Londoner Cyril Pullin, said that he had never had any problems, had only stopped twice in the 262-mile race – for fuel at the Rudge depot – and that the Multi was the best steering motorcycle he had ridden. It was capable of 80 mph on the level and averaged almost 50 mph for the entire race. This may not sound too impressive today, but the Mountain Circuit was little more than a gravel track in those days. Indeed, in the very early races the riders were actually required to dismount and open and close a sheep gate on each lap if no marshal was present to do it for them. Keppel Gate is still a well-known bend near the 34th milestone, but the gate has long since gone. One of the original stone gateposts still stands alongside the present-day marshals' hut.

The 1928 Rudge-Whitworth catalogue stated, 'We have concentrated the whole of our energy on ... the 500cc [size] and present to you three models; the Standard, the Special and the Sports.' It continues:

> Here then is your choice.
>   Reliability, power and 60 mph for £46
>   Grace, finish, reliability, power and 70 mph for £55
>   Acceleration, safety and 85 mph of breath-taking speed for £60

The machines had linked brakes operated by a foot pedal and a separate hand lever for the front brake only. The patented system was very sophisticated for its day, being

Above and right: The 500cc Rudge Special is a touring version of the sporty 'Ulster' model. The aluminium cover on the valve gear was introduced in 1937 and indicates that this machine dates from the final three years of Rudge production.

proportional in operation. When stopping gently, both brakes were applied evenly, but on harder braking the braking force at the front increased to compensate for weight transfer. There was even an optional extra (five shillings, or 25p in modern money) 'brake stop' to lock the brakes on when parking on a hill. The 'Patent Proportional Coupled' brakes were fitted to all models and became associated with the Rudge name long-term.

In that year, Graham Walker (whose middle name, Murray, was passed on to his son) won the Ulster Grand Prix at a record speed of more than 80 mph on a Rudge; to mark this – not to mention maximising the benefit from it – Rudge introduced their famous Ulster model for the 1929 season. Walker also became the company's sales manager at this time.

The Ulster was what would nowadays be termed a 'Race Replica', being very much a production model derived from the racing prototype. The single-cylinder bike had a four-valve cylinder head. Although the head was initially of a pent roof design, this was replaced by a radial valve layout for the 1932 season. Note that many Rudges were sold as 'fours', but this does not refer to the number of cylinders. It stands for 'four valve, four speed'.

For the 1930s, another 500cc machine was added to the Rudge range. The Special was a slightly de-tuned version of the Ulster, the original machine gaining a guarantee of a 100 mph capability. The Special had a lower compression ratio to 'soften' the engine, and together these two machines were to form the core of the range for the remainder of the decade. Lever operated centre stands were introduced in 1932, and from 1934 hand gear changes were replaced by foot operated gearboxes on all Rudge bikes. In 1937 the valve gear was enclosed. This latter change may not have contributed too much to out and out performance, but it made motorcycling a far less oily pursuit for both riders and passengers.

Rudge Whitworth were not immune to the difficulties of the Depression, of course, but the solution which enabled them to survive is arguably one of the less well-known aspects of their story. By 1933, the company was struggling and finding it hard to raise funds for the continued development of the Ulster. The Gramophone Company Ltd, later to become EMI, had always had a policy of diversification, and in 1936 they took over Rudge. In 1937 production was moved to the Gramophone Company works in Hayes, Middlesex. EMI retained the rights to Rudge until 1943, when they sold them on to Raleigh.

Smaller bikes also took their place in Rudge TT history; their 250cc machines scored first and second places in the Lightweight race in 1931, second and third the following year, and a clean sweep of the podium in 1934. A 250cc TT Replica was sold from 1932 though the primary chains of the road bikes were given oil bath cases.

The factory produced 250cc, 350cc and 500cc machines until 1939, when production ceased to allow EMI to focus on the electronic equipment, including the development and production of Radar, required for the war effort.

Raleigh

Raleigh are similar to many others in that they made their name as a bicycle manufacturer and then moved on to build motorcycles, yet different from most, nowadays they are really best known for their bicycles.

Frank Bowden made his fortune on the stock market in Hong Kong while in his twenties, but in 1887, when he was 38 years old, he was in such poor health that his doctor gave him six months to live. The doctor advised him to take up cycling for the sake of his health; he bought a tricycle from a small manufacturer in Raleigh Street, Nottingham. He was so impressed by it that he invested in the works, which was now renamed the Raleigh Cycle Company. In 1889 Bowden bought a controlling interest in Raleigh.

By 1891, having recovered his health and grown the business, Bowden needed a much bigger workshop; he left Raleigh Street but retained the company's name to commemorate its roots. Within six years Raleigh was the biggest bicycle manufacturer in the world and had become a public company. Bowden bought the company back in 1908, along with Sturmey-Archer Gears, and it was to remain under family ownership for the next 25 years.

Henry Sturmey and James Archer had each patented designs for three-speed hub gears, and it was Bowden who brought them together in 1903 and formed 'The Three-Speed Gear Syndicate', which became the Sturmey-Archer Gear Company in 1908. When Sir Frank Bowden, 1st Baronet of the City of Nottingham (conferred on him in 1915), died in 1921 at the age of 73, he was succeeded by his son, Sir Harold Bowden, 2nd Baronet.

It is worth attempting to clear up a common (and understandable) confusion at this early stage. The flexible cables used to control brakes, throttles, clutches and a number of other devices are known as Bowden cables and were used to replace the rigid brake rods on Frank Bowden's Raleigh bicycles from around 1902. It is commonly believed therefore that Frank Bowden invented the Bowden cable. The patent for the 'Bowden Mechanism' was in fact granted to an unrelated Irishman, Ernest Monnington Bowden in 1896. He entered into an agreement with the Raleigh Cycle Company, Lea and Francis Ltd, and the Riley Cycle Company on 12 January 1900, and from this point they all became members of 'E. M. Bowden's Patent Syndicate'.

Unfortunately, history is rarely quite that simple to unravel. Although the Bowden brake had been announced in the cycling press in the 1890s, it was claimed that it had not been used on cycles and an attempt was made in 1902 to patent a Bowden-type bicycle brake under the name of one George Larkin. There is documentation at the National Motor Museum, Beaulieu, to the effect that Larkin subsequently worked for E. M. Bowden as General Works Manager at Bowden Wire Ltd until 1917, the Syndicate having agreed to manufacture and market his design provided it was patented jointly under Larkin's name and theirs. At least we can be fairly sure that Frank Bowden didn't actually *invent* the Bowden cable.

By the early 1920s, Raleigh were producing not only bicycles in vast numbers but 15,000 motorcycles per year, along with 250,000 hub gears and 50,000 motorcycle

Above and left: The 350cc Raleigh Model 6 appeared in 1925 and when tested by the *Motor Cycle* it was described as a good handling machine, which went well without unpleasant vibration. It was found to have a top speed of 62 mph. The bike pictured dates from 1926.

gearboxes. The first Raleigh motorcycle was built in 1901, using a German-made 2-hp Schwan engine mounted above the front wheel. A much better and more reliable machine followed and G. P. Mills, the leading racing cyclist of his day, rode one from Lands End to John O'Groats in a time of just over 51 hours, experiencing no engine problems. This feat attracted favourable publicity as Mills was so well known, having won the inaugural Bordeaux-Paris bicycle race and set many cycling records, and also because his time beat not only the best previous cycle and motorcycle times, but was even two hours better than the car record. However, by 1906 trade in motorcycles had become very slow and the factory turned its full attention back to pedal cycles until conditions improved.

Motorcycle production restarted after the First World War and it was then that development really got started. Throughout the 1920s, Raleigh manufactured a range of machines powered by both side-valve singles and V-twins. They also supplied engines to many other firms, including Dunelt, Coventry-Eagle, Mars, Cotton and many others. There was a luxury 698cc flat-twin design with cylinders fore and aft à la Douglas, which was introduced in 1919, but manufacturing difficulties meant that this was fairly short-lived.

As the picture on p. 107 shows, there was also an overhead-valve single-cylinder engine which was available in 348cc and 498cc versions. Raleigh's chief designer during the 1920s and '30s, D. R. O'Donavan, was responsible for the successful Sturmey-Archer racing engines which were used by Raleigh and others.

There were further demonstrations of reliability between the wars, with Hugh Gibson riding a sidecar outfit around the entire British coastline, while Marjorie Cottle did the same in the opposite direction on a solo bike.

In 1933 motorcycle production stopped again, and bicycles kept the company safely in profit. Raleigh were able to ride out the Depression well, buying out Humber Cycles in 1932 and reverting to public ownership in 1934 with a share issue of £2 million (equivalent to at least £65 million today). This time, however, it was to be 25 years before any more powered machines were made, and they were not 'full-on' motorbikes.

In 1958 a moped, made by BSA and powered by a 49cc Sturmey-Archer engine, carried the Raleigh name. Throughout the 1960s various similar bikes were produced, including one built under licence from Motobecane. In the final analysis Raleigh are, as they always were, bicycle makers. However, unlike so many of their late nineteenth-century peers, they have continued to be successful bicycle makers. In the 1970s they achieved huge popularity – cult status, even – with the 'chopper'. And most of those carried a Sturmey-Archer three-speed hub gear.

Opposite below: Sturmey-Archer are best known for their hub gears, but this fabulous 496cc long-stroke single, powering Martin Stratford Parkson's equally fabulous 1930 Dunelt Drake, leaves no doubt of their wider engineering ability.

Chapter 7

Sidecars – Family Transport, Weapons and Racers

Nowadays we tend to take the car for granted. It seems as if everybody has one, or even more than one, but this is a very recent situation. Even as late as the 1960s, the recently completed M1 was a very quiet road and average middle class families were just beginning to think about buying a car.

Thinking back to my own childhood, I can remember the excitement when my older sister arrived home with her second-hand white Triumph Herald. I even remember the registration number and the dealer's name because it was a special thing. Yet it was not my first experience of powered transport as I had already travelled in the sidecar of my brother's BSA. Sidecars, of course, had been commonplace not just for years, but for decades.

A motorcycle is great transport for one. It can carry two when required, provided a pillion is fitted (and they weren't always, of course) but luggage is always a problem. When I tour on my modern Yamaha (yes, I admit it, and it's a great machine too) I carry all I need for anything up to a fortnight, but it isn't exactly convenient, and 'all I need' is inevitably determined in part by 'what I can carry'. Climbing on and off needs thinking about too as the years take their toll! If I were not travelling alone it simply wouldn't work.

One possible solution would be to tow a trailer. Motorcycle luggage trailers are legal up to a maximum width of one metre and must not extend more than two and a half metres behind the motorcycle's rear wheel spindle. They are not particularly popular in Britain but they do sell well in some parts of the world. Attempts have been made to use trailers to carry passengers as well as luggage, and I came across this little snippet on the internet one day (origin and truthfulness unknown):

> Way back in the early 1900's [sic] when motorcycles first hit the road, a trailer was used to transport a rider's lady friend behind his motorcycle. Because of poor hitch connections, the ladies were frequently lost....

Probably not the best way to keep your wife or girlfriend in those days then – metaphorically or literally.

A sidecar can be a simple platform for luggage, a more practical single extra seat, or a comparatively luxurious 'carriage' with a comfortable(ish) seat, a boot for the

The First World War Triumph Model H with wicker sidecar. (*Courtesy of Adrian Pingstone*)

luggage and even a roof to keep the rain off; for much of the history of the motorcycle, they have been the most affordable personal transport for the family man.

Adrian Pingstone's picture (above) of the Triumph Model H illustrates a beautifully simple and relatively low-cost method of constructing bodywork, which was popular around the time of the First World War. Such wicker-work bodies, using 'technology' effectively borrowed from the Bath chairs used by invalids, were tough and durable. They could withstand getting wet and needed little maintenance. They also had a degree of flexibility which was useful on the bumpy roads and tracks over which the machine would inevitably be driven. It obviously offered no weather protection to its occupant though – other than the invalid's blanket!

Riding a machine with a sidecar is quite different from riding a solo. Specifically, of course, the bike does not lean into corners, and inexperienced riders have often been 'caught out' by this. One very experienced motorcyclist of my acquaintance has told me that on his first sidecar ride he arrived at a corner, leaned – and went straight on into a neighbour's driveway. In fact, we never steer a bike by leaning, though many believe they do. The bike leans as it turns, but turning is initiated with the handlebars. What is different is the way the handlebars are used. On a solo motorcycle travelling at any speed above perhaps 20 mph, a technique known as 'counter steering' is needed. To turn left you push the bars gently to the right and this initiates both the turn and the lean. It is not the purpose of this book to argue with those who do not accept this, but it clearly doesn't work with a sidecar attached! At very low speeds the steering is similar to a solo bike, but at higher speeds it differs.

One problem which is common to all motorcycles and cars, but which has its most serious effect on motorcycle and sidecar combinations, is the tendency of the front end of a machine to 'dive' under heavy braking. This alters the geometry of the three-wheeled sidecar outfit and therefore affects the steering.

The English engineer Ernest Earles patented a design which eliminated dive and also enabled the wheelbase to remain virtually constant as the suspension moved. The Earles fork is a form of leading link, but the main fork is bent back so far that the moving link can be pivoted behind the wheel. How does this prevent dive? As the brakes are applied, there is inevitably a tendency for the drum (or disc) to rotate forwards with the wheel and this has to be prevented by a torque arm attached to the fork. On the Earles fork this torque arm can be attached in such a position that it lifts the fork. Careful calculation of the various angles actually enables dive to be reduced, eliminated, or even reversed so that the front end rises under braking! As mentioned, the chief advantage of this system is on sidecar outfits and the Douglas Dragonfly illustrates it perfectly. Russian-made Ural outfits use a leading link front suspension, but this is technically not an Earles fork as the pivot is not behind the wheel – the basis of the Earles patent. BMW used an Earles fork on solo bikes for many years, but these were designed to allow some dive as most solo riders prefer the greater 'feel' this gives under braking.

Whether or not the sidecar outfit is fitted with an Earles-type fork, another important braking issue arises from the mass of the sidecar itself. If the sidecar wheel is not fitted

This 1955 348cc Douglas Dragonfly sidecar outfit is fitted with an Earles fork. The linkage between the brake drum and the fork can be seen clearly. Of course the linkage is needed on a conventional fork to prevent rotation of the drum, but on an Earles fork it also prevents 'dive' under braking.

with a brake then the sidecar will tend to 'overtake' the bike and pull on the steering, a problem which naturally worsens if a passenger is actually being carried. Many sidecars are fitted with a brake for this reason. Of course, the pull is reversed under acceleration and there have been examples of two-wheel-drive outfits; notably such machines were built cooperatively by BMW and the Russian Ural Company during the early stages of the Second World War, though clearly this cooperation was not destined to be long lasting.

Cornering is also different on an outfit since the sidecar will act as a stabiliser when it is on the outside of the turn, but will simply tend to leave the ground when it is on the inside, allowing the bike to lean outwards. Adding a passenger greatly reduces this effect, so the sidecar rider/driver must now exercise greater care when the 'chair' is empty.

As sidecars were so popular in the early days, it naturally follows that many businesses found it profitable to make them. Some were motorcycle manufacturers who also made sidecars to fit their machines, but there were also specialist builders. Probably the best-known specialist maker of sidecars from the earliest times until the present day is the Watsonian Company, which was founded in Birmingham in 1912 by Thomas Fredrick Watson.

Watson himself, who was a builder by trade rather than an engineer, had been unwilling to leave his motorcycle and sidecar combination out in the street in front of his home, but was unable to get it through the narrow passage leading to the rear of his property without the lengthy process of unbolting the sidecar, and of course reattaching it the following day.

His response was to design and construct a folding sidecar which could be kept in place while still allowing the machine to be wheeled through the restricted entrance. He patented this invention in 1911 and found that others were interested in it. He is reported to have made a number in his own house, with his wife running up the upholstery on her sewing machine!

These were originally sold for 12 guineas† under the name 'The Patent Collapsible Sidecar Company Limited', but by 1912 the name was the more recognisable 'Watsonian Folding Sidecar Company', and by the early 1920s they had become the largest sidecar manufacturer in England, absorbing or simply closing down many of their competitors. At their height, Watsonian's share of what was then a very large market reached approximately 50 per cent, with sidecars rolling off the line at a rate of 200 per week.

The original market for folding, or collapsible, sidecars had actually been fairly limited, although quite a large number were sold for pedal cycles all the way through to the 1950s, by which time there was even a two-seater version suitable for tandems (sidecars had in fact originated as cycle attachments in the 1890s). As an alternative, the Kwik Fit chassis, which could easily be removed or replaced as needed, was introduced in 1926.

---

† One guinea was equal to one pound and one shilling. There were twenty shillings to a pound. Twelve guineas was a considerable sum in 1911. The original Triumph Speed Twin sold for seventy-four pounds twenty-six years later.

Advert for Watsonian sidecars.
(*Courtesy of Grace's Guide*)

However, the company's sales really 'took off' because at an early stage (prior to the First World War) more conventional wicker bodies joined the range. Watson's firm was well placed to supply sidecars during the conflict, and in addition to outright military purposes of transport, communication and fast attack, the company's products were found to be suitable for use as ambulances.

More elaborate coach-built bodies with ash frames and plywood panels came into their own soon after the war, and these traditional materials and methods, familiar to the users of horse-drawn carriages and soon supplemented by steel panelling, remained the basis of sidecar construction until they were finally replaced by Glass Reinforced Plastic (fibreglass) in the 1950s.

Various major structural changes to the company itself occurred over the years, including a simplification of the name – to simply 'The Watsonian Sidecar Company' – in 1930. On leaving T. F. Watson's house in 1912, a factory had been established in Balsall Heath, Birmingham, but this was also quickly outgrown. The next move was in 1922, to premises in Hockley, but these burned down in 1930 and Watsonian production moved to Greet. The most recent move was to Blockley, in Gloucestershire, in 1984.

Watsonian bought the Swallow Sidecars name – a remnant of the company which had long ago become Jaguar Cars – from Tube Investments in 1956.

Sales of sidecars continued to be strong until the early 1960s, but when cheap cars such as the Ford Popular and the Austin Mini arrived on the scene, large numbers of those who had previously ridden sidecar outfits chiefly for their advantages as economical and convenient transport began to buy cars.

Watsonian were just about able to survive this situation; they had established a forge for the manufacture of wheel braces and bottle jacks and probably more importantly they had developed a relationship with Land Rover, putting their experience and expertise in glass-fibre products to work for the larger business. When Land Rover withdrew from this arrangement Watsonian were in serious trouble. In the early 1970s they were producing very small numbers of sidecars and things looked bleak.

At this time, and completely independently, Peter Rivers and Mike Williams set up an engineering company, Squire, in Bidford-upon-Avon. The original purpose of the company was to do engineering prototype work and vehicle restoration, and they employed Harry Briggs to work on the restorations. Briggs had been the proprietor

Is this the lowest Vincent in the world? Because a sidecar outfit doesn't lean it can run with far less ground clearance and a correspondingly lower centre of gravity than a solo.

Another consequence of the lack of lean is the use of tyres with flat treads.

of the now defunct Briggs Sidecars, and he persuaded Rivers and Williams that there could still be a market for sidecars. However, they realised that the traditional market was effectively gone; what remained was a demand from enthusiasts for 'sports' sidecars rather than the traditional models initially favoured by Briggs. They built their own chassis and bought in fibreglass bodies.

Squire sidecars sold well but were not immune from the effects of recession in the 1980s. They were holding their own, but not thriving, and a meeting was arranged with Watsonian's management which resulted in an agreement to merge the two companies. By this time Watsonian, despite their fibreglass knowhow, were buying in their engineering requirements from outside, and so the two parties, Watsonian and Squire, brought interlocking skill sets to the new partnership.

The new company, Watsonian-Squire, was formed in 1989, at which point Squire moved their operations the 10 miles to the Blockley site. In 1999 Watsonian-Squire also became the UK distributor for the now Indian-made Royal Enfield motorcycles.

The sidecar has had other faces. In war there is an obvious need for transport; not only for guns and ammunition or even large groups of soldiers, but also for individuals. In both World Wars, reliable communication, for example, could still depend on men or women physically carrying messages from place to place since electronic methods could easily be disrupted. The motorcycle was small, light and relatively easy to maintain and it was widely used. In the First World War the Triumph Model H was used extensively by army despatch riders and over 30,000 were produced specifically for this purpose. It required virtually no modification to withstand the rigours of

The bonnet of a sidecar such as this Squire makes a useful autograph album! Some great names here too.

military life, although it was found that large bumps could cause breakage of the front suspension spring. Riders quickly began to add a leather strap as a form of 'bump stop', but that was about all that was needed.

The Motor Machine Gun Service was formed in 1914 during the early part of the war, when it was realised that batteries of highly mobile machine guns could be of real value. Each battery consisted of eighteen Clyno or Royal Enfield motorcycle/sidecar combinations carrying six Vickers Maxim machine guns and supported by eight solo Triumph motorcycles and a small number of cars or trucks.

The sidecar did not provide a stable enough platform for a machine gun and in order for it to be fired it was removed from the outfit and fitted to a tripod. A gun-carrying machine actually went into battle in company with two others without guns to carry fuel, ammunition and spare parts, and to provide backup if the lead machine broke down.

The Clyno Company had been in dire financial straits at the start of the war, but the War Office contract enabled the firm to survive for a time. However, they also entered into an agreement with the Russian government to supply mobile machine gun units as well as ammunition carriers and solos. Unfortunately for Clyno, these were never paid for and contributed in part to the company's demise soon after the war. Matchless, who were not given a contract with British forces, actually built 100 similar motorcycle/machine gun combinations for the Russian Army, but following the revolution in 1917 these were not delivered, and they eventually saw service with British troops. Alfred Scott was another who produced a machine gun carriage in the hope of a government contract, but this was not forthcoming.

In the Second World War, motorcycles again played their part. Many of the major manufacturers were there, with Triumph, Norton, Matchless, BSA, Velocette, James and Rudge all represented. BSA alone, as the largest manufacturer, supplied a total of 126,000 M20 machines to the British armed forces over the period including the war years.

As might be expected, the other British maker with its roots in armaments – British Enfield – also produced motorbikes for military applications, and these included the famous 125cc 'Flying Flea', which could be dropped from an aircraft in order to increase the mobility of airborne troops.

Despite having its factory destroyed during the blitz on Coventry, Triumph moved to premises in Meriden, and in addition to producing many thousands of bikes, also made aircraft parts, as had Clyno during the previous conflict.

Sidecar races were held at Brooklands from 1912 and the first sidecar TT on the Isle of Man was won in 1923 by Freddie Dixon and Walter Perry on a Douglas machine fitted with a 'banking' sidecar designed by Dixon himself. Interestingly, the idea of a sidecar race was originally resisted by many of the sidecar manufacturers, who regarded their products purely as family transport and felt that racing was an unsuitable and unsafe way to show them off to the public. Happily that first race at least was accident free, and sidecar sales were not harmed by the publicity.

It isn't just road racing which features sidecar outfits either. They are used in hill climbs, motocross, grass-track racing – in fact all kinds of motorcycle sport. There has been a world championship for sidecars since 1949, the first winners being Eric Oliver and Dennis Jenkins (of Mille Miglia fame) riding a Norton/Watsonian outfit. Some

Above and below: This 1962 BSA Goldstar based racing outfit tells its own story. 'The only Goldy ever to score World Championship Road Race points.' The bronze TT replica awarded for this performance is displayed along with the passenger's helmet.

1962 BSA GOLDSTAR
D.F. (FRED) BRINDLEY & JACK WAUGH
8th PLACE IN 1962 TT
THE ONLY GOLDY EVER TO SCORE WORLD
CHAMPIONSHIP ROAD RACE POINTS.
1963 TT CRASHED AT BUNGALOW.
1995 BARN FIND AND RENOVATED BY
ASH BROOKES.
BULMER CHASSIS.

would claim that the racing sidecar has lost its relevance nowadays since sidecars are no longer popular and the racing version bears no real resemblance to anything on the road, but when a vehicle of any kind is developed for racing it tends to leave its road-going roots behind. Just compare the modern Formula One car with even the fastest road car. Modern racing sidecars are among the most spectacular and highly evolved of all machines used in motorsport, and if you have yet to see them in action it is a treat which can be highly recommended.

In order to lower the centre of gravity the driver no longer sits astride the bike. In a modern racing outfit he kneels over the engine. The intakes are howling just a couple of inches below his chin and the rear wheel is between his knees. The 'passenger' is by no means just a passenger. It is his (or sometimes her) job to act as moveable ballast, leaning across behind the driver when the machine turns right (for an outfit with the chair on the left), often sliding at the rear like a fast car, and hanging off to the left to keep the chair wheel down – or at least close to the ground – on left handers. On the straights the passenger lies flat to minimise air resistance and tends not to even see where he or she is going. Handles are fitted in convenient places to enable all this movement and with speeds of around 150 mph being possible, it pays to keep a firm grip; certainly not a job for the timid.

While marshalling at Quarter Bridge on the Isle of Man, this author has seen the colourless face of a passenger whose driver had just clipped the kerb at the bottom of Bray Hill and all but thrown him off. They sat down together for a while before even making it across the road to the pub. Names have been withheld to protect the innocent and the guilty!

Sidecars race off-road too....

Chapter 8

Two Become One

AJS

The Stevens brothers, Harry, George, Jack and Joe, set about manufacturing motorcycles under the name AJS soon after the turn of the twentieth century, their Model A appearing in 1910. The name AJS was apparently taken from Jack's initials since he (full name Albert John Stevens) was the only one with a middle name! Their father, Joe Senior, who had begun as a blacksmith, was a gifted engineer and the Stevens Screw Company had a firmly established reputation for quality. He had experimented with motorcycles even earlier, using a Mitchell engine imported from the USA in 1897. The family not only improved on the Mitchell design, but by 1909 they were supplying 125cc twin-cylinder power units, of both parallel and Vee layout, to several manufacturers. It was when a machine fitted with a Stevens side-valve engine won a 24-hour non-stop trophy competition that Jack Stevens decided he wanted to enter the Isle of Man TT; this in turn led to the formation of the new company.

AJS Motorcycles were based in Retreat Street, Wolverhampton, and the Model A's engine capacity was set at 298cc so that it would be eligible for the Junior race at the TT, which at that time was limited to machines of less than 300cc. The bike was exhibited at the 1910 Motorcycle Show and performed creditably on the Isle of Man in 1911; Jack finished 16th on the factory entry, with the similar but privately owned machine of J. D. Corke just one place ahead.

Demand for the factory's products precluded entry in the 1912 event, but in 1913 they achieved a 10th place. Real success began in 1914, with the regulations for the Junior now changed to allow engines up to 350cc, and the AJS not only enlarged to 349cc but also sporting a four-speed gearbox and chain drive. A strong team of AJS bikes were entered and the Stevens family were rewarded with first, second, third, fourth and sixth place finishes.

Demand increased again; this time to such an extent that the old works could no longer meet the company's requirements. They moved to new premises on the outskirts of the town, reconstituted the firm as A. J. Stevens (1914) Ltd and added an 800cc (or 6-hp) V-twin to the existing 2¾-hp Model A.

In November 1916 the Ministry of Munitions prohibited the production of motorcycles for non-military purposes, but AJS were fortunate enough to gain part of

The 350cc side-valve engine was a mainstay of the AJS range in the 1920s.

an order to supply the Russian government with military equipment which kept the factory in work until the prohibition was lifted following the Armistice.

In 1920 AJS machines gained internal expanding brakes and chain primary drive – the link between the engine shaft and the gearbox – and AJS rider Cyril Williams won the first postwar TT. 1921 provided a bit of TT history, being the first year in which the Senior TT was won by a 350cc bike. The bike, of course, was an AJS, the rider on this occasion being Howard R. Davies, whose initials are now permanently associated with Vincent bikes.

Two new models were introduced in 1928. These were the 349cc K7 and the 498cc K10, and both were overhead camshaft racers. The M7 and M10 appeared in 1929 and the works riders were a pair of true greats, Wal Handley and Jimmie Guthrie. How many teams have had corners on the TT course named after *both* their star riders? Handley's is a highly recognisable left/right turn alongside a high stone wall between the 11th and 12th milestones, and Guthrie's is a fast right hander on the way up the Mountain which top riders regard as one of the most important to get right on a fast lap. Next to the Marshals' post there is a monument to Jimmie Guthrie, who died in the 1937 German Grand Prix, and a bench next to the course in

The exposed kickstart mechanism of a 1928 AJS J12.

Douglas describes Handley as 'one of the bravest who ever passed this way'. He died in the Second World War while delivering aircraft as a member of the Air Transport Auxiliary. Handley finished second in the 1929 Junior and Guthrie won the 1930 Lightweight on a 250cc AJS.

The AJS S3 went into production in 1931. This was a 496cc transverse engine V-twin tourer with shaft primary drive and alloy heads. It was an expensive design both to develop and to manufacture. This would have been fine if it had sold like hot cakes, but sadly it didn't and the AJS Company were soon in financial difficulties. Before the year was out they were bankrupt and the assets were bought by the Collier Brothers, owners of Matchless, and by the car maker Crossley Motors. Motorcycle production left Wolverhampton and moved to Plumstead, and in 1938 AJS became part of Associated Motorcycles, a management company set up by the Colliers to handle their expanding interests. From this point, Matchless and AJS shared models, distinguished only by their badges and colour schemes.

There is one 'shared' machine that commands the highest level of respect among all lovers and racers of classic machinery. In 1948 Europe was beginning to recover from the horrors of war and the economic mess of the Depression which had preceded it. Motorcycle racers were beginning to return to their sport and AJS decided to produce a bike which would be good enough to give an account of itself in International events, yet affordable for serious (i.e. pretty well off) amateurs.

They had plenty of experience with overhead cam singles and they also gave the new engine a few features 'borrowed' from the Velocette KTT; the bore and stroke

The 350cc AJS 7R, resplendent in black and gold.

were the same as the KTT at 74 mm x 81 mm, giving 350cc, and also the eccentric adjustment of the single large inlet and exhaust valves. Nevertheless the new AJS 7R was a much more advanced machine than the KTT. The frame was an up to date all-welded design with a swinging arm rear and good powerful brakes.

Many parts were fabricated from an alloy of magnesium known as elektron, which was developed in Germany during the First World War. Intended to replace aluminium alloy, elektron weighs slightly less than two thirds as much. Being magnesium it also burns ferociously and is very difficult to extinguish and has been used to make incendiary bombs, but some versions also have high tensile strength and are suitable for use in aircraft and other areas where lightness and strength are essential – such as racing cars and racing bikes.

The 7R used elektron engine casings and brake drums. The engine castings were anodised gold and immediately gave the bike a recognisable 'look'. The completed bike weighed in at slightly less than 300 lbs (136 kg) and the engine gave 30 hp.

Continuous work by development engineer Jack Williams eventually raised this to almost 42 bhp, but the 7R was competitive and reliable from the outset. It was never really to be a force at the very highest level, although Les Graham used it to win the 1950 Swiss Grand Prix. Overall the bike proved itself to be, as was intended, a solid and quick machine for the ordinary racer; it quickly earned the title 'The Boy's Racer'. In 1958 AMC performed one of their best known pieces of badge engineering and produced a 500cc version under the Matchless name, the equally famous Matchless G50. Most purists now regard the 7R as the last true AJS motorcycle.

Above: In 1948 AMC joined the 500cc vertical twin club, producing the AJS Model 20/Matchless G9. These were gradually increased in capacity and replaced in 1961 by the still very similar 650cc Model 31/G12 pairing. The picture shows a *c.* 1961 Model 31.

Opposite above: AJS 16M. The letter in the model name was used to denote the year of manufacture – in this case 1950. This 350cc machine is stated to be in 'all original' condition. It differs from the Matchless G3 only in minor detail – the G3 has its magneto mounted behind the cylinder barrel for example.

Opposite below: The beautiful AJS 7R on track at Jurby.

In spite of the above, this author feels that one other AJS deserves to be mentioned here, rather than be enveloped by the AMC mantle. The E90 Porcupine was a pure-bred Grand Prix machine and was introduced at the 1947 TT, some years after the Stevens family lost control of the AJS name. There was no road bike equivalent for the public to buy and consequently very few were made. Yet the Porcupine carried the AJS name to the 1949 500cc World Championship and was the only twin-cylinder machine ever to do so.

The E90's two parallel cylinders were positioned horizontally, facing forwards, in order to lower the engine's centre of gravity, and the head had distinctive 'spikey' fins which explain the 'porcupine' tag. Note that I *will* go along with the purists by not confusing this bike with the 1952 E95 Porcupine which was a different and less successful bike with the same nickname; it didn't even have the spikey fins.

The E90 was originally conceived in the last years of the Second World War by AMC designer Vic Webb and Joe Craig, more normally associated with Norton, and was built with assistance from Phil Irving, who was also a member of AMC's development team by that time. It was intended to compete with the supercharged multi-cylinder

This 350cc Model 7 AJS dates from around 1930 and is equipped with a 'Brooklands Can' silencer to comply with the regulations of the time.

machines which had begun to outclass the British singles in the immediate pre-war years. Craig and Webb believed that it was pointless to generate massive power if this was done at the expense of excessive weight, resulting in an unwieldy motorcycle which was difficult to ride. They set out to design a lighter, yet still powerful bike using a supercharged parallel twin; the horizontal cylinders provided space for a supercharger above the unit construction gearbox. Unfortunately for this plan, supercharging was banned in racing after the war and the engine had to be adapted to run with normal aspiration.

Many years later, ex-AJS works rider Ted Frend, who had been the first rider to win a race on the bike, was reported to have said that carburation was the biggest problem they experienced with the engine, and this presumably reflected the loss of the intended 'blower'. Nevertheless, the porcupine was quick enough to win, and in 1949 Les Graham (another rider commemorated on the TT course) beat Italian Nello Pagani to the inaugural 500cc World Championship by the narrowest of margins. Pagani actually scored more points than Graham, but under the rules of the day, a rider only counted his best three scores and Graham had two wins and a second place. Pagani had two wins and a third and so Graham was the champion. This was both his and AJS's only major championship; Graham sadly was killed riding an MV in the 1953 Senior TT. The Graham memorial takes the form of a brick and timber shelter between the Verandah and the Bungalow on the Mountain section and is used as a marshalling and medical point.

Matchless

The Matchless Motorcycle Company was the trading name of Collier and Sons, having been founded in Plumstead, London, in 1899 by Henry Herbert Collier and his two sons Charlie and Harry. The brothers were to become major players in the British motorcycle industry as they later bought out AJS from the Stevens family and set up a parent company, Associated Motorcycles (AMC), which was eventually to include Norton, to manage a group of manufacturers.

Matchless, with its winged 'M' logo, was one of the companies whose name became celebrated in large measure due to the racing successes of their products. In fact the single-cylinder race at the first motorcycle-only Manx TT in 1907 was won by a Matchless – and what's more the rider was Charlie Collier.

In 1910, Charlie lapped the Brooklands circuit at 80.24 mph and raised this to 91.37 mph the following season. The brothers experimented with three- and six-speed gearing using combinations of epicyclic gears similar to those used on high quality bicycles such as the Sunbeam and double-pulleyed V-belts.

The first Matchless machine went into production in 1901 using engines from De Dion Bouton among others. These machines were essentially bicycles with a small single-cylinder engine hanging in front of the downtube and driving the rear wheel by a long belt, independently of the pedals.

A V-twin bike was produced (with a JAP engine) in 1905. Harry Collier won the 1909 TT and Charlie was successful again in 1910. Records were set at Brooklands and Matchless products were rapidly established as one of the most successful and desirable motorbikes of this early period.

The youngest Collier brother, Bert, also became active in the company as chief designer at an early stage and was to fulfil this role until the Second World War.

By 1912 Matchless were making their own engine, a 3½-hp 500cc design with an almost 'square' bore and stroke (85.5 mm x 85 mm). Producing engines in-house was often a good sign that a manufacturer meant business, and over the next 20 years the company made both singles and twins in sizes from 500cc to 1,000cc.

The Model 7 was a two-speed 8-hp machine with a twin-cylinder 770cc engine – either JAP or Collier/Matchless – which used pedals to start it. This may or may not have been easier than the more common starting handles of the period. The lower gear was provided by an epicyclic gear set in the rear hub, which was activated by a friction belt. The drive was transmitted to the rear wheel by belt. These were prone to slipping or breaking, particularly when working in combination with larger engines, but Matchless provided at least a partial solution by using a pair of belts. Not only did they slip less, but if one broke you could still get home.

When the First World War began, Matchless were ready with a military model but they were not awarded a contract to supply motorcycles to the British. A few do exist with 'War Model' stamped on the crankcases. Could at least some of these be from a batch originally intended as machine gun carriers for the Russian army? It is after all known that they were never delivered and that they eventually saw service with British forces.

In the absence of a War Department order, the factory spent the war years making accurately machined parts for weapons and aircraft (which of course came to the fore for the first time in this conflict). The model originally intended for military service was renamed the 'Victory' model when peace returned.

The Model H appeared in 1920 and was similar in layout to many other machines of the time, having an essentially bicycle-like frame with a flat tank and a very basic, undamped girder fork. However, an early form of swinging arm type rear suspension was fitted. It was powered by an inlet-over-exhaust MAG 1,000cc V-twin of Swiss manufacture, and had an automatic valve lifter connected to the kickstart mechanism (itself still quite a novel fitment).

If a sidecar was desired the chassis was available with a fully integrated chair chassis. Indeed, some models were only made available with sidecars, a decision which may well have been unique to Matchless.

A review in *The Motorcycle* of 1 December 1920 reported that the Matchless had 'given unqualified satisfaction during the last 12 months' and the reviewer was pleased to note that few changes had been made for 1921. Later Model H machines also used JAP engines and the type continued in production until 1927.

Patriarch H. H. Collier died in 1926 and the firm became a limited company within a couple of years. In the years 1930 and 1931 Matchless changed their tank badge from the full company name to the famous silver 'M' (though without wings) and introduced two major models – the Silver Arrow, designed by Charlie, and Bert's Silver Hawk. At least they should have been of major importance if quality of design and build coupled with a high specification were enough. But this was the 1930s.

The Matchless Silver Arrow was powered by a 397cc side-valve narrow angle V-twin developing 16 bhp. The advantage of the narrow 'V' was the ability to fit a one-piece cylinder head. Initially the Arrow was fitted with a three-speed Sturmey-Archer gearbox, although this was replaced by a four-speed in 1933. The chassis had been designed to use a sloping engine, since this was what the fashion-conscious buyer was demanding at the time. It used a cantilever rear suspension with a pair of springs under the saddle in a fashion reminiscent of the later Vincent-HRD, and friction dampers were fitted as was common at the time, but these were fitted with an adjustment knob which made them capable of being adjusted while riding. The bike also had innovative linked brakes. The brake pedal operated both brakes, but the handlebar lever was connected to the front brake only. Additional luxury features included enclosed valve gear which did not coat the rider's trouser legs with oil, dry sump lubrication and a side stand. The bike was also beautifully smooth-running and easy to start.

Unfortunately, the 1930s was the time of the Great Depression. In fact, the expensive Silver Arrow was introduced shortly after the New York Stock Exchange crash, and even with the 1933 upgrades the bike never really had a chance of long-term success. A total of about 1,700 were built before the Arrow was withdrawn from the catalogue.

In 1931 the economic situation had another even bigger effect on the British motorcycle industry when the long-established AJS Company of Wolverhampton failed and the Collier brothers bought the factory and rights from the Stevens family. From this time on, AJS and Matchless machines became so closely related that many AJS enthusiasts regard later AJS models as no more than badge-engineered Matchless bikes.

Bert Collier's Silver Hawk shared many elements of the earlier machine's design. Again it was a smooth, quiet, narrow angle (26°) 'V', but the capacity was now 592cc and again the cylinders were contained within a single casting and topped by a one-piece head, but this bike was intended to compete with Ariel's Square Four, and it had gained the extra two cylinders to become a V-Four. The Hawk engine benefitted from overhead cams and the camshaft was driven by a shaft and bevel gears. A four-speed gearbox was standard, but the engine was so tractable that it could run comfortably in top gear all the way from walking pace to 80 mph. This engine started so easily that the starting lever could apparently be operated by hand and no valve lifter was fitted.

Again, however, the economic climate was too great an obstacle and the Hawk, whose production costs must have been considerably greater than those of the Square Four, was dropped in 1935. Nevertheless, this sophisticated bike played its part in establishing Matchless as one of the major British manufacturers and became the basis for the AJS V-4 some years later.

Although 1935 saw the sad demise of the Hawk it also saw the beginning of the immensely successful G series. Although the public, apparently then in a conservative mood, had influenced Matchless design in the 1920s and early '30s by refusing to let the trusty side-valve engine go completely, most G models were fitted with the more modern and efficient overhead valves.

In 1938 the company grew even larger as Sunbeam joined AJS under Matchless ownership; it was at this point that the Colliers changed the name again. Associated Motor Cycles Ltd (AMC) was born and the 'M' badge sprouted wings.

As the Second World War loomed, the company were, this time, asked to produce motorcycles for the armed forces; their response was the G3, of which some 80,000 were ultimately supplied. This bike remained in use with the Army even after the war, and was still in production into the 1960s. The original specification included girder forks, but the popularity of the design increased when AMC's damped telescopic forks (which they called 'teledraulic' forks) were substituted in 1941.

The new version, known as the G3/L – the 'L' standing for 'Lightweight' – was introduced in response to the War Office's requirement of an off-road machine. The 'L' variant was some 56 lbs (25 kg) lighter than the standard G3, but of course it would regain a lot of weight when carrying its load of military equipment. A trials machine based on the G3/L would later achieve a great deal of peacetime competitive success.

Triumph's 350cc vertical twin, the faster and even lighter 3TW, actually won the War Office competition for this order, but Triumph's Coventry works were completely destroyed in a German bombing raid in November 1940 and so the contract went to Matchless anyway. The Matchless factory's entire capacity was dedicated to production of the G3/L from 1942.

The G5 model was available in both 350cc and 500cc versions, the larger machine being additionally named the 'Tourist'. There were also 'Clubman' (trials) and 'Clubman Special' (scrambler) variants.

With the war over and normality beginning to reassert itself, AMC introduced a new and successful Matchless trials machine based on the G3/L, but with increased ground clearance, reduced weight and competition tyres. 1948 saw the debut of the G9, a 500cc vertical twin with swinging arm rear suspension and distinctive, rather fat, oil-filled dampers. The appearance of these units quickly earned the bike the nickname 'Jampot' which has stuck (excuse the pun!) to the make ever since. Indeed the Matchless Owners Club magazine is called *The Jampot* to this day.

The racing version of the G9 was the G45 and this went into production in 1952 following Derek Farrant's win in that year's Manx Grand Prix. This event was – and still is – the amateur equivalent of the Isle of Man TT. It is held later in the year on exactly the same course and has often proved just as influential as its better known sister event.

The company produced the G11 in 1955 and also acquired James, Norton and Francis-Barnett. As with AJS and Sunbeam, these companies maintained their separate identities in the short term but were inevitably absorbed within AMC over time. Of the three, Norton is the only one which has retained a strong profile in the public consciousness. Even in 2012 a Norton-badged Senior machine was able to create a stir of excitement on the Isle of Man. The engine was an Italian Aprilia and the Senior TT race was cancelled due to poor weather, but the bike was sent out to perform a display lap for the public, standing around the course in the rain to see it; such is the remaining power of the Norton name. Having been there at the time, I will admit that the bike not only looked like a Norton, it had been made to sound pretty much like a Norton too.

Only 180 Matchless G50 racers were actually made by AMC over a period of just four years, yet the single-cylinder overhead cam 500cc G50 (50 bhp) machine is perhaps one of the best known bikes to bear the company's name (or the winged 'M' for that matter). Replicas continued to be made after AMC went under, and indeed new G50s can still be bought. The bike is an enlarged development of the 350cc AJS 7R, having the same 78-mm bore but an increased stroke of 90 mm, and on first glance only the paint scheme distinguishes the two machines. On second glance that remains true. AJS machines display the old Sunbeam heritage of black and gold which goes all the way back to James Marston and his training as a Japanner in Victorian Wolverhampton. The Matchless models got two paint options – red and black with gold engine cases or bright blue with a tan seat and gold engine cases. The G50 was less powerful than the Manx Norton, but was nevertheless competitive due to its lighter weight which helped it in the corners and compensated for the lack of power under acceleration.

The bike was not initially accepted for American racing as it was not based on a production motorcycle and so Matchless introduced a street-legal machine by fitting the G50 engine into a scrambler frame. These bikes were sold under the name G50 CSR, with the added letters standing for Competition Sprung-frame Roadster. However, it soon became known as the Coffee Shop Racer, although this may have been intended to be derogatory. It was also sold under the name 'Golden Eagle', presumably because of those instantly recognisable gold cases. Only twenty-five G50 CSRs were built and all were exported to America – for perhaps obvious reasons. Ironically enough, rumour has it that quite a few were immediately cannibalised so that their engines could be used for racing!

When AMC ran into financial difficulties and ceased production in 1963 the tooling and spares for the AJS and Matchless bikes were bought in 1966 by Colin Seeley, an ex-sidecar Grand Prix racer who had become one of Britain's best designers of motorcycle frames. He has continued to produce Seeley AJS and Seeley Matchless machines up to the present day.

There was also a final fling for Matchless courtesy of businessman Les Harris, hailed in the 1980s as 'the saviour of the British motorcycle industry'. After being granted a licence to produce Triumphs for five years, and having done so, he set out to produce a machine of his own.

The Harris Matchless G80 was produced by L. F. Harris from 1987 until 1990, when economic conditions brought the venture to an end. Harris and his wife Shirley, a partner in the firm, then returned to their previous core business supplying parts for classic motorcycles. This G80 was powered by an Austrian-made Rotax 494cc air-cooled engine and in its final form boasted a twin front disc brake and electric starting. The Rotax engine found its way into another 'revived' machine of that period, the Cotton LCRS.

The 494cc Rotax-engined Matchless G80 was produced from 1987 to 1990 by L. F. Harris.

Chapter 9

Ariel and BSA

Ariel

Starley and Hillman had established the Ariel Cycle Company in the nineteenth century, but they had long since gone their separate ways by the time the first Ariel motorcycle rolled out of the factory. In the late 1880s the company had become part of Rudge-Whitworth, itself a combination of several smaller firms, and the Ariel name fell into disuse, but came into the ownership of the Dunlop Company.

In 1896, Dunlop began manufacturing bicycles under their own name and naturally fitting them with their own patented pneumatic tyres, but this caused disquiet among other cycle manufacturers. Why? Because the tyres were patented and everyone had to buy them from Dunlop! In effect the bicycle makers were now being forced to buy tyres from a direct competitor – and advertise his wares into the bargain.

The objections were sufficiently strong to make Dunlop decide that something had to be done, and they looked around for a new name for their cycle division. The Ariel name was already associated with Dunlop tyres due to the use of Dunlop rubber on Starley's bicycles, and as they now owned it, this was the name chosen. The (new) Ariel Cycle Company was established at this point, but it was not retained for long by Dunlop. In 1897 a disparate group of companies known as Cycle Components Manufacturing acquired Ariel from Dunlop, moving it to Dale Road, Bournbrook, South Birmingham. It was from Dale Road that the first Ariel motorcycles emerged.

In fact the first motorised Ariel was a not a bike, but a trike. This appeared in 1898, and the first powered two-wheeler followed three years later, fitted with a 211cc Minerva engine. Over the next few years the Ariel range grew to include middle sized and larger machines, including an occasional V-twin, but most of these were powered by proprietary engines or at least engines designed by other companies and manufactured by Ariel under licence. A good example is the White and Poppe 482cc side-valve unit which was used in most of the early singles. It was originally bought in ready built, but was made under licence right up to 1926. Other engines came from MAG and JAP while many of the V-twins were by AKD.

Things really changed when star designer Val Page arrived in 1925. He revolutionised the model range, designing a modern overhead-valve engine with hemispherical combustion chambers as his first major project for the company. The engine was developed over a two-year period and in 1927 it was fitted into a newly designed frame. This all-new bike was to be worth the wait, ultimately becoming the Red Hunter line which remained in production until Ariel ceased four-stroke manufacture in 1959.

Edward Turner joined the company in 1929 and his extremely successful Square Four made its debut in 1931, initially as a 500cc machine and enlarged to 600cc for sidecar use in 1932. Ariel were now a thoroughly revitalised motorcycle company, but as Britain entered the financial Depression of the 1930s, they struggled, along with everyone else.

By the end of 1932 the company's well-founded hopes had crashed down about them through no fault of their own. Ariel was bankrupt and that would have been the end of the story were it not for the faith of their managing director Jack Sangster who invested his personal wealth into the company, enabling it to reopen under the name Ariel Works (JS) Limited.

The company now operated from a small part of the original factory and a much-simplified range was produced. In fact, although a variety of models of varying specifications and engine sizes of 348cc, 497cc and 557cc were listed, there were only two basic engines since the 350 was just a 500 with a smaller bore. What is more, all the bikes used the same frame; a highly economical solution in desperate times!

Ariel's 348/497cc engine owed its final form to both of their important engineers. The original design was of course by Val Page – whose Mark V single was later to be transformed by Edward Turner into the basis of the Triumph Tiger – but it was Turner who took Page's 1931 497cc large-valve ohv single and combined it with the same designer's 1932 crankcase and timing chest.

The bikes were produced in two-speed, three-speed and 'Red Hunter' versions; the Red Hunters had a distinctive and stylish red and chrome tank designed by Turner.

The long-lived and rightly admired Ariel Red Hunter. The 'VH' variant was a 497cc model, produced from 1945 to 1958.

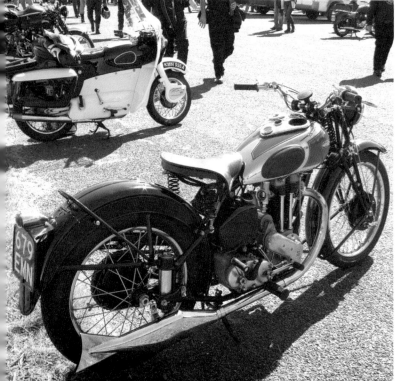

Above: Edward Turner's classic Ariel engine was the Square Four.

Left: The machine in the foreground is a rather older version of the 497cc Red Hunter, while a two-stroke Leader can be seen behind with its pressed steel frame. Possibly best described as 'ahead of its time', the Leader was also available in stripped-down Sports forms as the Arrow and Golden Arrow models.

Opposite above: Val Page's overhead-valve single-cylinder engine is a true design classic.

Opposite below: This 347cc 'NH' model has much more of an off-road feel.

All buyers of the 500cc Red Hunter were actually provided with two pistons giving a choice of compression ratios; the lower (giving 6.8 to 1) was for road use and the higher for competition. The high compression piston gave a top speed above 90 mph.

Although George Formby took a somewhat disguised Red Hunter to a Senior TT victory in the film 'No Limit' the Red Hunter was not a major success in road or track races. Its competitive reputation was, however, more than taken care of in trials events. The legendary Sammy Miller won so many awards with his 497cc machine that even its registration number (GOV 132) became famous.

So strong was the original design that few changes were made over the years. A review in *The Motor Cycle* (26 July 1951) suggested that 'the manufacturer is not suffering mechanical bothers' and that 'their model is proving popular with the public', adding that 'the Red Hunter's all-round performance is most satisfying'.

A particular strength of this motorcycle was its ability as a sidecar machine. Indeed, the Red Hunter remained almost the only way to go in sidecar trials right up to the 1970s. It also saw military service in the Second World War, when detuned Red Hunter engines were fitted into Ariel trials frames. The last road-going versions were built in 1959.

BSA

Following the outbreak of the Crimean War in 1854, new machinery had been introduced from America to boost production at the Royal Small Arms Factory at Enfield. So successful was this move that British gunsmiths found their livings

Above left and right: A neat and carefully thought out linkage enables the plunger rear suspension unit of the Red Hunter to move vertically without binding. Compare this with the equivalent components of the 'Garden Gate' Norton – which was prone to breakage.

under threat. The increased mechanisation at Enfield had reduced reliance on skilled craftsmen.

A group of fourteen members of the Birmingham Small Arms Trade Association sought, and received, access to the technical drawings and other facilities of the Enfield factory, and in June 1861 the company that came to be known as Birmingham Small Arms, or simply BSA, was formed.

The Enfield machinery brought a new and important engineering concept to Birmingham – that of interchangeable parts. Although the company gained large orders for weapons, including the Lee-Metford rifle, with which the entire British Army was re-equipped in 1887/8 at a rate of 1,200 rifles per week, there were also lean times for BSA. During the worst of these, in 1879, the factory was closed for the entire year. However, it was able to reopen in 1880 as a bicycle factory and the story of the BSA board's conversion is worth telling in itself as it sounds very much like an episode of a popular modern television programme.

Mr E. C. F. Otto had invented a new type of bicycle, the 'Dicycle', which had one large wheel on each side of the rider. He claimed that this was a more stable, and therefore safer machine than the high wheeler (or penny farthing), which people were then injuring themselves on. He is reported to have demonstrated his invention by riding it up and down the boardroom table, before leaving the room and riding it down the stairs and out into the street. The directors were suitably impressed and BSA entered the road transport business. They were, of course, well placed since large-scale bicycle manufacture calls for large quantities of components to be machined accurately and at low cost. BSA had the required facilities lying idle.

It was in 1881 that BSA finally registered the stacked rifles symbol, previously used in their advertising, as an official trademark. It rapidly became famous around the world. In fact, bicycle production may only have been seen as a stop-gap until the arms trade picked up again. In any event it stopped when the Lee-Metford order came in.

In 1893, after the contributions of Robert Thomson, John Dunlop and Charles Goodyear had together made cycling both more comfortable and popular, a partial restart occurred, initially with bicycle hubs (actually made by a machine formerly used to make artillery shells!) and then of other components for the cycle trade. Complete bicycles were not made again under the BSA name until 1908, but three years prior to that an experimental motorcycle had been built. The frame was BSA's own design and the engine was a 233cc Minerva similar to those used in the early Triumphs. The frame was made available to the motorcycle trade and a prototype BSA engine was tested although this was not followed up openly at that time. Development work did continue in the background, however, and as a result the 498cc 3½-hp model, when it appeared at Olympia in 1910, was an immediate success. BSA's classic and very beautiful forest green colour scheme with gold pin-striping also made its first appearance either at the Olympia Show or soon after.

When BSA formally diversified into motorcycle manufacture in 1910 they were already well placed to occupy a position as a major player. They had several decades of engineering experience, were well financed and owned well-equipped modern premises whereas many of their competitors were newly formed companies operating on a very much smaller scale. An additional advantage was that as gun makers, they were accustomed to working to exacting standards. The workforce at BSA rapidly gained a reputation for producing high quality cycle and motorcycle parts too. It therefore comes as no surprise that they rapidly gained a large market share. In fact, they were ultimately to become the biggest motorcycle manufacturer in the world.

That original BSA motorcycle seen by the public at the Olympia Show and available to buy in 1911 had a sturdy frame and a double sprung fork and was considered to have a good level of performance. A rear wheel clutch was available as an extra and the complete machine sold for £50.

Prior to the First World War, development continued. There was the 557cc 4¼-hp long-stroke Model K with a three-speed chain and belt combined drive and the similar Model H, which was well ahead of its time in having all-chain drive. Everyone seems to have produced a Model H at that time; answers on a postcard? BSA also added well-constructed sidecars to their motorcycling range.

Everything changed with the arrival of the war. An average week had seen 135 guns produced by the BSA factory on Armoury Road. During the four and a half years of the war, 1½ million rifles were made along with 145,000 Lewis machine guns and vast amounts of ammunition. There were also motorcycles, bicycles, machine tools and aircraft components. BSA had bought Daimler in 1910 and this arm of the rapidly expanding company supplied staff cars, ambulances, commercial vehicles and even engines and gearboxes for the first tanks. By the end of hostilities the workforce had increased from 6,500 to over 20,000 and the total length of BSA's production lines exceeded two miles.

The giant company was separated into three divisions when peace returned, and BSA Cycles Ltd took control of cycle and motorcycle production at BSA factories in Small Heath and Redditch.

At this stage the BSA group looked strong, but peacetime conditions did not support the company's wartime size, and by 1921 only half of the 1918 workforce was still employed. Nevertheless, the motorcycle side of the business continued to do well, with the slogan 'One in four is a BSA' almost certainly correct. In a single twelve-month period in 1923/4 it was reported that they sold 26,000 motorcycles. Indeed, during the total period in which BSA made motorcycles, they made more than all the rest of the British industry put together.

The 1925 250cc Model B was easily recognised in the showroom or on the road by its distinctive round fuel tank, which also won it a choice of nicknames – simply the 'Round Tank' or in some quarters the 'Flying Marrow'! The bike was light, strong and economical. Powered by its little side-valve engine and offering only two gears, it was capable of just 45 mph and had no front brake, but it was keenly priced at slightly less than £40 and it sold brilliantly. Mass production 'assembly line' techniques were brought into the motorcycle division for the first time, and in all, some 35,000 Round Tanks (or Marrows) were sold in the relatively short production time of only four years.

In the early 1920s an ex-Daimler engineer, Harold Briggs, joined the BSA design team and quickly made his mark. He was responsible for the first overhead-valve BSA, the L28, which was added to the range in 1924. The 350cc single-cylinder engine

The Model G's 770cc V-twin was intended for sidecar use and this one still has an original (and well loaded) BSA two-seater sidecar attached.

(bore and stroke 72 mm x 85.5 mm) was a spin-off from the Hotchkiss unit with which Briggs was familiar and which was also used to power the BSA Light 10 car. The engine had fully enclosed valve gear with automatic lubrication; we take this last for granted now, but early riders were expected to operate hand pumps to feed oil to their engines. These 'total loss' systems lubricated the engine first and the road second and many were fitted with 'sight feeds' so the rider could actually see that his/her engine was getting its oil. The L28 not only retained sight feeds but also included a hand pump for 'emergencies', which could reputedly include steep hills.

The maximum power output from the engine in 'sports' trim using the optional high compression piston has been reported to be around 13 bhp, giving it a top speed of 60 mph. Note that the nominal power of an engine of this size for tax purposes was only 3½ hp. If the claimed brake horsepower figure is correct, it certainly shows just how quickly the 'tax' calculation was overtaken by advances in engineering.

In the months leading up to the war, BSA engineers had been working on a V-twin project, but this was suspended when hostilities began. However, its revival meant that from 1919 BSA were able to respond to the arrival of large numbers of war veterans with experience of motor cycle transport. They rapidly produced the confusingly named Model A V-twin (sensibly renamed the Model E from 1921) designed to be used with a sidecar, which they also manufactured. This was the first of a line of BSA bikes of this type and had a 771cc engine rated officially at 6 hp. Later superseded by the more powerful 986cc Models F and G, the Model E featured a three-speed BSA-made gearbox and an aluminium chaincase. The front and rear wheels were the same size and were interchangeable so that a spare could usefully be carried in the sidecar. The wheels even had dummy belt rims. At first glance this would seem obvious as part of the requirement for interchangeability, but the bike was of course chain driven. The actual purpose of these dummy rims was to provide surfaces for the brakes to operate on.

The engine was a 50-degree Vee as the BSA designers had decided that this was a good compromise. It gave adequate space between the cylinders for cooling purposes, but allowed a shorter wheelbase than the 90-degree layout considered ideal mechanically. The emphasis was on torque (for sidecar pulling) and reliability, together with ease of maintenance. The machine was a success and its descendants continued in production until the outbreak of the Second World War.

The Light 6, introduced in 1923, was a budget version of the Model E with various components lightened or removed in order to reduce production costs. However, the lower weight made it popular as a solo machine and it outlived its heavier brother (now referred to as the 'de luxe' model) by two years.

Among all Briggs models, the 'Sloper' stands out. Correctly and prosaically known as the S31, the machine marked a slight change from BSA's normally conservative design philosophy. They sold motorcycles to the large numbers of riders who looked at, and talked about, innovative sports bikes, but most of them actually bought practical machines combining reasonable performance with reliability, economy and ease of maintenance. BSA machines were well specified and up to date but they did not often cause a stir.

The Sloper, launched in 1927 for the 1928 season, did set a new trend. Unlike most previous machines, its single-cylinder 493cc overhead-valve engine leaned forward in the frame, allowing the saddle tank and seat to be set lower, producing a genuinely sleek appearance. This layout proved so popular that almost all manufacturers were soon forced to adopt something similar. Internally the S31 gained from Harold Briggs' experience at Daimler and featured wet sump lubrication – no more 'oiling the road' for BSA owners. This bike was so well loved that it continued in production until 1935, gaining extra chrome and a 595cc engine in 1930. Harold Briggs sadly died young, in August 1929, aged 33.

It has been stated often in this book that racing was always considered virtually essential to the development of good motorbikes and that winning was necessary to sell them. BSA could be seen truly as the 'exception that proves the rule'. They did compete in many events of different kinds but relied more heavily on demonstrations such as the demanding tests of standard machines which led to them receiving the Maudes Trophy in 1926, 1938 and 1952. In achieving these awards they demonstrated their ability to build a complete machine under observed conditions from standard spare parts bought all over Britain. Such machines started at the first kick and ran perfectly. This ready availability of quality spares was seen as more valuable to their customers than race wins.

Yet the top management certainly did believe that winning was the only way to race. In 1921 a works entry was made in the Isle of Man Senior TT. No fewer than fourteen special 500cc TT bikes were prepared for a mass assault. Six top riders were engaged to ensure success. The bikes were extensively tested at Brooklands to ensure reliability and they were painted resplendently in BSA green and cream and shipped to 'The Island'.

Above and below: By 1927 BSA had decided to concentrate on building possibly unexciting but highly reliable bikes, appealing to the average rider. This long-stroke side-valve machine was one of these.

Above and opposite BSA then had a partial change of heart and introduced saddle tanks and sloping engines! Soon everyone else was following BSA's lead. This is an S30, *c.* 1930.

Unfortunately in motorsport winning is never a 'given', and so it proved. The Brooklands tests, tough as they were, had not simulated the punishing conditions encountered in a 226-mile TT. The bikes did not handle well enough on the twisting Manx roads; in fact one of the riders, Gus Kuhn, was sidelined by injuries during practice week. Not one of the machines that started the race even made it half way. Some suffered valve failures and others melted their pistons; the incident shook BSA. They had nothing further to do with road racing – and the Isle of Man in particular – for many years.

Even as late as the mid-1950s, the BSA board were extremely wary. The 1954 MC1 racer was in a sense 'the BSA that never was'. Often when people see it they react by saying 'Is that really a BSA?' since the engine has a very un-BSA appearance. In fact in this author's opinion the whole machine bears more than a passing resemblance to an AJS Porcupine, with its single forward-facing cylinder (with two exhausts and two carburettors making it look like a twin) and its huge 7-gallon fuel tank ensuring that the bike looks a lot bigger than it is.

In fact it's tiny. An out and out 250cc racer with an ultra-light Reynolds 531 frame (*see Glossary*). The swinging arm monoshock rear was pretty adventurous in 1954 and the Earles-style front end gave handling which impressed no less a rider than Geoff Duke when he tested the bike at Oulton Park. Designed by Bert Hopwood and Doug Hele, the MC1 seemed to need only a better gearbox and brakes to be a potential world beater.

So why didn't it carry the world before it? Apparently the BSA board were reluctant to allow the machine to carry the firm's name. Duke was keen to race it on the Isle of Man and offered to call it the Geoff Duke Special. There was also a suggestion of calling it a Rudge, since this name was owned by BSA at the time, but ultimately the board said 'No'. Duke has since been quoted as saying that this decision convinced him that it would be a waste of time having anything further to do with BSA. Strong stuff, but did the board's rejection simply reflect BSA's fear of repeating their traumatic 1921 experience?

The Depression affected BSA, of course, but the company policy of building straightforward and well-engineered machinery meant that they not only survived but came through the 1930s in a strong position.

In 1936 Valentine Page moved to BSA from Triumph, where he had worked with Edward Turner on the design of the vertical twin and several important single-cylinder bikes. Page revised and simplified the existing BSA model range, advising on the removal of machines that were no longer economic to produce and improving those that were. In 1937 he designed the M23 Empire Star, which not only proved very successful in both 350cc and 500cc versions, but also gave BSA machines a new and distinctive shape. Developments of this classic were to remain in the catalogue all the way to the 1960s, and it was an Empire Star on which Wal Handley won

his Brooklands Gold Star, giving rise to the most famous BSA model name of all. Production of the BSA Gold Star began in 1938.

By the time the Second World War broke out, BSA were the largest motorcycle company in the world. This was the period in which they bought Sunbeam from AMC and in total they now owned sixty-seven UK factories. This time the BSA board had seen the war coming and had taken steps to ensure that they were prepared. Two executives attended the Leipzig Fair in 1935 and on their return they reported that war was inevitable. The board agreed a massive programme of expenditure which meant that, even without government backing, the planning office and tool room had already been on overtime for three years by the time Neville Chamberlain was forced to announce that the Second World War had begun.

As in the previous war, Birmingham Small Arms now produced a vast quantity of weapons and ammunition; almost half a million Browning guns and ten million shell fuses. Among this torrent of military equipment were more than 126,000 motorcycles, almost all of them M20s. By the time peace returned, BSA had added both New Hudson and Ariel to their group, and a few years later, in 1951, they bought out Triumph too.

The single-cylinder four-stroke 350cc B31 of 1949, though introduced after the Second World War, was essentially a pre-war design and had a solid rear end combined with telescopic forks at the front. It was capable of about 70 mph. By 1951, the Gold Star variant had a plunger frame. It also had a 500cc alloy engine and was capable of well over 100 mph. In fact, by the mid-1950s such bikes were able to lap the TT course at more than 85 mph average speeds. Bear in mind that this is a 37.75-mile circuit of closed public roads, passing through towns and villages and close to the exposed summit of Snaefell mountain. Even today it poses a unique challenge, but roads were much poorer in the 1950s.

The 1961 650cc Golden Flash has a much more modern-looking swinging arm rear suspension. The A10 (along with its 500cc smaller brother the A7) was a parallel twin and was produced over a 17-year period with the first A7 arriving in 1946, and the last A10 model (the Super Rocket) remaining in production until 1963.

Both were originally available in rigid and plunger versions, but rigid frames were phased out across most of the BSA range by 1952, with just a few single-cylinder models still managing without rear suspension after this time. The Golden Flash gained its swinging arm in 1954, and along the way it also gained a headlamp nacelle, bigger brakes and an Amal Monobloc carburettor (*see Glossary*).

The A10 Super Rocket was the last of the BSA pre-unit twins; that is to say, bikes with a separate engine and gearbox.

The Golden Flash in particular was also a popular sidecar machine due to its smooth and generous power delivery and brakes which were considered strong in their day. Magazine testers stated that the brakes could easily stop the machine from high speeds. This author's own recollections of a late-model A10 were a little less reassuring, but of course then, as now, condition is all and I was an impecunious student. The rear brake pedal was on the opposite side of the machine from the actuating lever on the drum, and this necessitated a cross shaft through the frame which was prone to damage if the machine was dropped – very difficult to remove if

The 600cc M21 was the postwar successor to the M20, which had been made in huge numbers for the military. In its turn, the M21 became a common sight fitted with a yellow 'AA' sidecar.

bent too! Somehow though, I can't see or hear one without thinking 'I used to have one of those', and that's how we really know how good an old bike was.

One of the BSA bikes pictured (p. 146) has a sidecar (note the leading link front suspension – 'almost' an Earles fork) and 'Kliktronic' push-button gearchange (*see Glossary*). Luxury.

Despite its 'British bike' appeal it has to be admitted that the original 125cc BSA Bantam was a direct derivative of the German DKW RT125 whose plans came to Birmingham in the aftermath of the Second World War. Nevertheless, in numerous forms the Bantam was in production from 1948 to 1971, a period of 23 years, and in its later revisions at least it had developed a character all of its own.

The original DKW-derived Bantam of 1948 was termed the D1. It had a 125cc engine, integral three-speed gearbox, and a 'hard tail' which is of course just the nice way of saying it had no rear suspension. At the front, however, the DKW's girder fork was replaced with a pair of telescopic legs. Ignition was provided by a Wico-Pacy or Lucas magneto and the bike was painted a drab colour termed 'mist green'.

These bikes were a great success, selling in large numbers to both the general public, for whom other transport options were limited by austerity following the war, and to the GPO (General Post Office) who used them for telegram delivery.

In 1954 the D3 model appeared, offering slightly more power from its enlarged 150cc engine and plunger rear suspension. The D1 continued in production in GPO trim (now with plunger suspension added) all the way to 1968. The D3 gained a swing arm in 1956.

The 175cc engine made its appearance in 1958 in the D5 model and the bike's physical appearance was updated with the D7 the following year. At this point, BSA

Above left and right: The Amal Monobloc and Concentric carburettors were the main methods of getting fuel into British engines for a great many years.

Opposite above: This Golden Flash is fitted with a leading link fork for sidecar work and also has a Kliktronic gear change system.

Opposite below: This road/race 1951 ZB34 Goldstar illustrates the period in which BSA moved away from solid rear ends to plungers. Swingarms were still to come.

seem to have preferred odd numbers for some reason, but in 1966 they had a change of heart and announced the D10. Power was now up to 10 bhp and the D10 'Bushman' was an off-road version with chunky tyres and extra ground clearance provided by a high-mounted engine and exhaust. These models also benefitted from coil ignition.

The four-speed box arrived on the D14/4 along with a distinctive two-tone tank and the final model (anomalously called the B175) was only a slight revision, offering such things as stronger forks (borrowed from the more powerful 250cc four-stroke C15), a stronger kick-start and a main beam warning light. Early models had a solo sprung seat and a parcel carrier. The modern foam-filled seat with room for a pillion passenger arrived as an option on later D1 models and was standard on the D3.

The author's first bike was a 175cc Bantam D14/4. This was chosen in 1972 from the used stock at Horner's in Manchester with the help of a more experienced friend. Always a good idea if you're only seventeen and/or don't know what to look out for. Mine left the factory in 1968 and it made a great introduction to biking. I took it to the Isle of Man and had my first (scary) taste of the TT course, and I rode it to school and imagined I looked super cool.

The D14/4 really was quite a different bike from the 1948 original. The gearbox had an extra ratio (hence the '/4'), the bike had larger diameter forks at the front and swinging arm rear suspension. It had more power than any previous Bantam – now up to 12½ bhp. It had a claimed top speed of 65 mph. As I hinted above, there are corners on the TT course that can't be taken that fast, and maybe it was going even faster downhill. The speedometer was swinging to and fro so I couldn't say. I did once try to improve its performance by increasing the ignition advance a bit, and for a few minutes the result was amazing; but then it seized, so I reset it to standard. It has to be said that the engine didn't seem to take any harm from this youthful mistreatment so it must have been pretty tough.

The Bantam was not only good for learning to ride, but also easy for a beginner to work on. The engine was an extremely basic two-stroke single with an integral clutch and gearbox and the whole thing was light enough to carry upstairs and strip down on a table in my bedroom. I had a very tolerant mother.

The bike was rather fussy about perfect ignition and carburation setup, so I got plenty of experience in those areas. The carb was an Amal Concentric (*see Glossary*); a wonderful and deceptively simple design which was found, in various sizes and with appropriate jetting, on a huge range of British motorcycles of the period. Later when I moved up to a 650cc BSA A10 Super Rocket, many things were different, but the familiar old Concentric was still there. Odd really, since the bike should have been fitted with the Amal TT, but then, other parts were non-standard too. The tank was a rather beautiful glass-fibre version originally fitted to an A65 Spitfire and the exhausts were straight-through racing megaphones. This bike was *loud*, but as a teenager I thought it sounded great – at least after I got the mixture adjusted so it stopped back-firing every time I rolled off the throttle.

The Bantam not only sold in good numbers right from the start, it inspired many owners to make modifications in order to seek a bit more performance. This inevitably also lead to competition; something the original designers in Germany presumably did not have in mind. Nevertheless, Bantam-based racing remains strong even to the present day.

Bantam-based racers bear little outward resemblance to the standard models. Hand-made expansion box exhausts mean that they sound aggressively different too. Such a system is designed to create a pressure wave which 'rams' unburnt mixture back into the cylinder. This only works over a very narrow rev band but gives a sizeable increase in power. Such pipes have to be tuned in both shape and length to give the maximum power boost and to give it at the most useful engine speed. It also makes for an engine which is difficult to use efficiently. Anyone who has seen two-stroke racing is familiar with riders slipping the clutch out of slow corners in order to keep revs up and get the engine 'on the pipe'.

This exhaust tuning has also resulted in many modern bikes having six gears. The two-stroke race bikes of the 1960s used large numbers of gears to make better use

Opposite above: The 1968 D14/4 was a far more refined machine than the original Bantam but the engine had changed little. Its capacity had increased over the years from 125cc to 175cc, but it remained instantly recognisable to the eyes and the ears.

Opposite below: The C15 was the learner-legal 250cc four-stroke in BSA's range.

Above: The DBD34 was the ultimate evolution of the Goldstar. A 499cc single, with 110 mph performance and stunning good looks, it was the BSA of choice among the café set.

Below: This 1961 650cc BSA A10 takes us close to the end of the pre-unit era.

of their narrow power band and rules were introduced to limit them to six. In fact, the competitive advantage enjoyed by Scotts in the 1920s still applies. A two-stroke engine fires once every revolution, as opposed to the four-stroke's once every two rotations, and can therefore produce more power.

As a result, the two-stroke was dominant in racing, where ultimate performance is everything, until very recently. Two-strokes held sway in the MotoGP class, the pinnacle of motorcycle racing, until 2002 when the rules were changed to favour four-strokes. In a move which Alfred Scott would certainly have recognised, the four-strokes were given a capacity advantage. This time, however, the advantage was great enough to ensure that two-strokes could no longer compete. Two-strokes retained their existing limit of 500cc and four-strokes were allowed up to 990cc. The following year there were no two-strokes in the MotoGP field.

They did continue in the 125cc Grand Prix class right up to 2011, but again the rules were used to remove them as the class itself was replaced by Moto 3 – a series for 250cc four-strokes. The most likely reason for this apparent antipathy to a design which demonstrably produces more power than a four-stroke is that it is seen as having little or no relevance outside racing. The two-stroke tends to be noisy and unreliable and must inevitably burn its oil, and so the four-stroke has retained its position as the engine of choice in most non-racing applications. Many enthusiasts lament the passing of the 'stroker', and with the development of solutions to its problems it remains possible that Scott may have the last laugh.

Returning to our story, a desperate shortage of vehicles worldwide meant there was a postwar boom in the motorcycle market and in 1953 BSA Motorcycles Ltd was formed as a separate business from BSA Cycles. At this time virtually all parts of the BSA conglomerate were thriving as the world sought to rebuild itself after six years of destruction. The BSA organisation consisted of nearly thirty companies, all operating separately but under the overall control of one giant company. About the only component not profitable was luxury car maker Daimler, and they were sold, enabling Jaguar Cars to expand.

In 1961, 100 years after the foundation of BSA, confidence was high and further acquisitions were still being made. Yet somehow it all began to go wrong, and when it went wrong, it went astonishingly quickly. From a profit of £3.5 million in 1960, trading had declined at such a great rate that by 1970 a loss of £8.5 million was recorded. BSA Motorcycles were experiencing problems as potential customers turned away from the newest models. The company's bankers provided a £10 million rescue package and a new Chief Executive, Brian Eustace, set about organising the fight for profitability.

There were now redundancies throughout the group; assets were sold and so were some of the smaller peripheral companies. In 1971 no less than thirteen new motorcycles were announced in measures that were starting to appear rather frantic. It didn't work. Losses continued to mount and by the end of the year bankruptcy loomed.

Associated Motor Cycles had already been bought by Manganese Bronze Holdings and now a deal was arranged which saw BSA join them in a new company to be called Norton Villiers. The BSA model line did not form part of the plan, and so the production of BSA motorcycles ended with almost startling suddenness in 1973.

Chapter 10

Triumph and Norton

Triumph

In 1886, a pair of German immigrants, Siegried Bettmann and Mauritz Schulte, renamed their London-based company the Triumph Cycle Company and in 1888 they established a factory in Coventry. The first Triumph motorcycle rolled out in 1902. One of the best known British motorbike manufacturers was thus born of German parents.

The Model H was a big success for Triumph, being adopted by the military for service in the First World War. Triumph were already producing their own 4-hp 550cc engine and their machine also had 'proper' front suspension. Telescopic forks and shock absorbers were still in the future, but a D-shaped 'girder' pivoted at the head bearing acts on a spring between the handlebars. This crude arrangement results in a considerable change in the geometry of the bike as the suspension moves – even the wheelbase varies greatly – but developments of the girder system, removing such shortcomings, remained in use for many decades. Indeed, Phil Vincent (of whom much more later) continued to reject telescopic forks into the 1950s. The Model H was used extensively by army despatch riders in the First World War and over 30,000 were produced for this purpose.

The Model H also used a chain-driven Sturmey-Archer three-speed gearbox with a hand operated lever. These gearboxes were to be popular in many motorcycles of the period, and were even used by the Brough Superior. The bike in the picture opposite has a leather belt around the headstock. Army riders commonly added these to prevent breakage of the spring on rough ground.

Edward Turner, Bert Hopwood and Val Page

A trio of really influential names these. Valentine (Val) Page, born in 1892, served an apprenticeship with J. A. Prestwich and was then employed with them as a designer. His engines were among those used by George Brough in the immensely famous (and immensely expensive) SS100 and SS80 'Superior' models.

Above and below: This Model H Triumph dates from 1912 and was therefore celebrating its centenary in Britain's triumphant Olympic year. Its owner referred to the bike as the 'Oil'ympic Triumph!

Leaving JAP in 1925, Page moved to Ariel as chief designer and was joined in 1929 by the 28-year-old Edward Turner. Turner had already designed several engines and had even built a complete motorcycle – The Turner Special – using his own patented 350cc overhead-cam single-cylinder engine, whose gear-driven valve arrangement allowed the head to be removed without disturbing the valve gear. Other major components used on this machine included a proprietary girder fork by the Webb Company, who supplied forks to Veloce for many years, and a Sturmey-Archer three-speed gearbox.

The Turner Special was registered for road use and was listed in the February 1927 *Buyer's Guide* with a price tag of £75, but only the original prototype is known to have existed.

When Turner joined Ariel he brought with him the drawings for an unusual 'square four' engine. These had already been rejected by BSA but were viewed more favourably by Page, and presumably by Ariel's boss Jack Sangster. What could have been the BSA Square Four was therefore to achieve long-term fame under the Ariel name.

This engine was effectively a pair of 250cc vertical twins built one behind the other in a common block and crankcase and with their cranks geared together to give 500cc in total. After the first year's production, the machine's capacity was increased to 600cc and this was further increased to 1,000cc in 1936.

Such layouts tend to suffer problems with vibration. For an extreme example consider the BRM H16 Formula One car engine, introduced in 1966. This was an attempt to build a 3-litre engine relatively quickly following the change from the old 1.5-litre Formula. It was powerful and hugely fast in a straight line, but rarely finished a race due to the vibrations.

Fortunately, Turner and Ariel were not thinking in terms of a high-performance machine, and the 'Squariel' was so popular that it remained in production for 28 years. In total, almost 16,000 Square Fours were manufactured and Turner's position was established.

Meanwhile, Page had not been idle, having designed the highly successful and long-lived Red Hunter, and a young Bert Hopwood had also been making his mark at Ariel. This company may be seen as one of the true 'centres of excellence' in motorcycle design long before any such term had been dreamed up. Hopwood was to go on to work for Norton, BSA and Triumph, and his path would frequently bring him back into close contact with Turner and Page.

Page left Ariel in 1932 and moved to Triumph, again as chief designer, but after four years he moved on again, this time to BSA. Almost immediately, Triumph decided to separate the car and motorcycle aspects of their business and sold the motorcycle arm to Sangster. He renamed it 'Triumph Engineering Company' and appointed Turner, now thirty-five, as general manager – complete with a 5 per cent commission on net profits – and chief designer! One can only imagine how Page may have felt about this turn of events. Bert Hopwood was also hired at this point as Turner's design assistant.

In fact, given his existing achievements, it is remarkable that Turner's main claim to fame was yet to come. It was his association with Triumph that truly was to make him a household name – at least among motorcyclists.

He rapidly set to work revamping the range, initially redesigning the 250cc, 350cc and 500cc singles with new frames, more modern enclosed valve gear, fresh paint and more chrome. These updated machines were marketed as the Tiger 70, 80 and 90, the numbers approximating to their top speeds.

However, it was in July 1937 that Turner introduced his great masterpiece. Any consideration of British motorcycle engines rapidly turns to the Triumph Speed Twin. The concept of a 500cc four-stroke overhead-valve twin was not new. The frame into which this engine was originally bolted had a rigid rear end and a girder fork. And yet this machine transformed Triumph's fortunes and gave a whole new image to 'British bikes' – the image which remains strong to the present day both here and abroad.

Although not revolutionary in concept, the Twin had more power and torque than its competitors. Turner understood that for a given engine size, multiple lightweight pistons moving more quickly mean more power. In effect this is similar to the two-stroke advantage. A high-revving engine gets the fuel in, burned and out again more quickly – and it also runs more smoothly.

It was also lighter and relatively easy to start. This latter was an important consideration at the time. Modern riders, used to simply switching on, pressing a button and riding away can have little idea of the joys of a kick-start. Once mastered it could look simple enough, but do it wrong and you could get a serious kick, an

Pre-unit Speed Twin engine in custom frame (hence the high exhaust pipe).

By 1959 the Speed Twin had gained the unlovely 'bathtub' fairing.

injured ankle and quite likely drop the bike into the bargain. There are painful-looking examples to be seen on the internet of riders attempting to start classic machines without previous experience. A bike which spun easily and started first time was a real luxury.

The Speed Twin even looked good; Turner retained and indeed enhanced the character of the popular singles. The engine has clean, elegant lines and conforms to the old engineering maxim 'if it looks right, it is right'. The Speed Twin looked right from day one.

Although introduced in 1937, the Twin made its real impact after the war. Triumph's factory was destroyed on 14 November 1940 in the Coventry blitz, along with a great deal of tooling and paperwork, and a new plant was built in Meriden. By the end of the war, Triumph had supplied some 50,000 machines to the military, but it was the revamped Speed Twin which enabled the company to thrive in the postwar years.

For 1946 it gained telescopic forks and an optional sprung hub at the rear, and in this form it produced 28 bhp and weighed 182 kg (400 lbs). This gave a lively performance with a top speed of around 100 mph depending on conditions. The sprung hub was itself a Turner invention. It was fairly heavy and allowed only a small amount of undamped travel, but could be fitted to the existing rigid frame without the need for modification.

Turner did not see the Speed Twin as a racing machine. In its earliest form the engine barrels were secured to the crankcase by six studs and nuts, but when owners took to tuning and racing the bikes (as it was, of course, inevitable they would!) this was found to be a point of potential weakness and so later models had eight studs. This may have been the origin of Turner's objections. The Twin was designed as a reliable road bike and increasing its power could lead to loss of this reliability, and this could perhaps damage a machine's reputation.

There is a story (quite possibly apocryphal) that Turner found a couple of Triumph apprentices adding a supercharger to their bike and stood over them while they smashed it with a sledgehammer. But he could not prevent private owners pursuing such projects, of course, and by the end of the 1940s other companies were building 500cc twins, so the Speed Twin engine was given a larger bore and stroke, increasing its capacity to 650cc. Turner named this more powerful machine the Thunderbird and for a time it was the fastest bike in the Triumph line-up.

The early Twins had a separate engine and gearbox. This was replaced by a Unit Construction machine in 1957. There was also a Sports version, the Tiger 100, from 1959, the '100' again representing its top speed. When an engine of 650cc was fitted the bike became the Tiger 110.

The TR5 Trophy was an off-road variant; its name was derived from the manufacturers' team trophy won by a trio of the machines in the world famous International Six Days Trial. The 650cc TR6 Trophy was added to the range in 1956.

The 750cc T140 Triumph Bonneville and TR7 Tiger are really very similar bikes, the Bonneville being a twin-carburettor version of the Tiger. These machines were produced by the Meriden Cooperative following the collapse of Norton Villiers Triumph in 1977. The two in the pictures (pp. 159 & 160) both live in Germany and are the property of Guenter Kranz, who like so many vintage bike enthusiasts, owns a collection of several machines. In Guenter's case the collection is fifteen strong and includes no fewer than three Manx Nortons, one of which ran in the 1994 Manx Grand Prix. Guenter, who also owns a staggeringly well-equipped workshop and has a wealth of racing experience, reports that he can feel no difference in power between the two 750cc Triumph engines.

Points of interest on this pair even include the number plates. The 07- number on the Tiger indicates a vintage vehicle and attracts a lower tax rate in Germany. Unlike British plates these also indicate that the vehicles are registered to an owner who lives in Bad Tolz, Bavaria, and that the Bonneville has passed its MOT-equivalent safety inspection. This is the upper of the two badges on the left of the plate (the brown colour even indicates that the most recent test was in 2010). The Tiger doesn't need one as it was first registered in 1980; ie., more than 30 years ago. The other badge is the Bavarian registration seal. Helpfully, the plate on the non-vintage machine has been kept small by the practice of deliberately allocating single letters and small numbers (T78 in this case) to the lower row when registering motorcycles.

Above: Wobbly Bob's (real name Bob Taylor) T100 Scrambler.

Left: Another Bob Taylor machine, this replica of 'Slippery Sam' draws a crowd wherever he parks it. Sam was the most famous of all Triumph Tridents – a three-cylinder 'Speed Twin-and-a-half' – and won no less than five consecutive Production TTs. The original was destroyed in a museum fire.

Opposite above: In common with other machines of its era (such as the Royal Enfield Bullet and the 'cammy' Norton) the Speed Twin was fitted with a visual gear indicator. It's still not obvious why….

Opposite below: Guenter Kranz's Tiger 750.

Above left and right: German number plates are highly informative.

Les Harris

Les Harris was a businessman based in Torquay who earned himself the accolade
– from the press at least – 'saviour of the British motorcycle industry' in the 1980s.
When the Meriden Cooperative failed in 1983, the Triumph factory faced closure.
Bids were invited and Harris was among those who attempted to buy the rights to the
Triumph name. He did not succeed, but approached the winning bidder, John Bloor,
with a proposal to manufacture the 750cc Bonnevilles (and the single carburettor
750cc Tigers which were used by the Royal Signals' 'White Helmets' Motorcycle
Display Team) under licence.

A five-year agreement was hammered out and Harris moved to a new factory and
warehouse. As a result, Triumph can claim to have been in continuous production of
motorcycles since 1902 and to be the oldest surviving continuous manufacturer. This
enables Triumph fans to dispute a similar claim for Royal Enfield – each manufacturer
naturally has its adherents!

The Harris-built Triumphs actually contained far more foreign parts than any
previous versions. The Brembo brakes were Italian, as were the Paioli forks and
Lafranconi exhausts. Switchgear and horn were of German origin. The sad truth is
that the British motorcycle industry had shrunk to the point where it was no longer
possible to source such parts at home.

When the five-year licence expired, Les decided not to extend it, but designed his
own motorcycle, which sold for a time as the Matchless G80. He died in 2009 and
the White Helmets provided a 'throttle roar' at his funeral in memory of the man who
had built their bikes.

Above: The classic elegance of the Bonneville T120 from around 1966 – though the fuel tank is understandably a more recent replacement.

Below: The style of the original twins can still be discerned in the most modern Triumphs.

Norton

James Lansdowne Norton formed his company in Birmingham in 1898 to make bicycle chains and soon realised the potential of the newly developing motorcycle. By 1902 the company had gained a contract to supply frames for the Clement-Garrard powered bicycle. Norton produced his first complete motorcycle, the 145cc Energette, in 1902, using the same French-made Clement engine which his customer Charles Garrard had been using. The engine naturally fitted his existing frames, not that this would be a complex problem since the engine was simply attached to the front downtube of the diamond frame with the fuel tank suspended from the top tube. By 1908 the energetic entrepreneur Norton was already manufacturing his own engines.

The Energette engine drove the rear wheel by means of a belt and a pair of pulleys, while conventional bicycle pedals helped it out on hills and were also used for starting. The pedal mechanism included a freewheel so that the rider could rest from pedalling on level ground.

The 1929 600cc Norton Model 19. This engine was a version of the firm's first overhead valve unit which was originally designed by James Norton himself.

The Norton name is therefore one of the oldest of all in the motorcycle world and the firm also has an immensely strong racing pedigree, having been entering machines and winning races in the Isle of Man TT since the event became a 'motorcycle only' race in 1907, right up until the 1990s. The first win came in that 1907 TT with Rem Fowler, mounted on a 684cc Peugeot-engined Norton, taking victory in the multi-cylinder class at an average speed of 36.22 mph, despite coming off on lap seven at the 'Devil's Elbow' section on the coast road. The course did not include Snaefell in that first running as the single-speed and virtually brakeless bikes would have had great difficulty going up and probably even more coming down. The course ran from St Johns to Ballacraine, turned left onto the modern TT circuit, and followed it as far as Douglas Road Corner on the way into KirkMichael where it turned left again and followed the coast road back to Peel and St Johns. The lap was 15¾ miles in length and the riders completed ten laps. Such was the pace of development in those early days that when the course was used for the last time (only four years later) the fastest lap was completed at an average of 53.15 mph.

In the 1930s Nortons won many TTs, and Norton riders such as Jimmie Guthrie and Stanley Woods were household names, just as Jorge Lorenzo and Valentino Rossi are today. The 'Manx' Nortons were tuned versions of the Norton International model (also known as the Model 30 or the 'Cammy') and were powered by an overhead cam single-cylinder engine of either 348cc for the Junior class or 499cc for the Senior. A double overhead cam version appeared in 1937 and this engine, developed for racing by Norton's engineer Joe Craig, was to remain fundamentally competitive for many years.

Rex McCandless and the Featherbed Frame

Rex McCandless is one of the most famous names in the classic motorcycle world. He was a completely self-taught engineer who had left school in 1928 at the age of 13 with no formal qualifications. He read widely in the engineering field but always preferred to learn first hand. He managed to transform the fortunes of one of the biggest and most famous motorcycle manufacturers and produce a racing machine in 1950 which spawned a massively successful road bike which is still available in replica form from numerous makers today. Wherever enthusiasts gather with their bikes, several of these will be based on the McCandless 'Featherbed' design.

He attributed his interest in mechanical things generally and motorbikes in particular to a 1923 side-valve Raleigh given to him by an aunt. Once into his twenties, his job at the Belfast aircraft company Short and Harland enabled him to buy a new Tiger 100 which he tuned and took racing, winning the Irish 500cc Road Race and Hillclimb Championship in 1940. Despite this he saw himself as primarily an engineer, regarding his brother Cromie, nine years his junior, as the better rider. Cromie justified his brother's faith in him, going on to ride in 500cc Grand Prix events and winning one (the Senior Ulster Grand Prix) in 1951. He was also to join the exclusive ranks of TT winners that same year.

et

Rex did not restrict his interests to motorcycles alone. His friend Artie Bell, who became a top rider and was eventually employed by Norton, ran a garage on Cregagh Road, Belfast (now a carpet warehouse), and there is a story that one of Bell's mechanics used to refer to McCandless as a 'mad inventor' who would sometimes stay on the Bell premises overnight, forgetting to eat, as he attempted to solve engineering puzzles which may even have involved autogyros. One of his best-known sayings 'When you solve a problem you haven't got one' would seem to typify this dogged determination to get things figured out.

The autogyro is a one-man helicopter of the type seen in the 1967 James Bond film *You Only Live Twice*. It uses the principle of autorotation, which is used by pilots of conventional helicopters in emergencies following engine or tail rotor failure. The rotor is disconnected from the engine as soon as engine revs drop below rotor speed and the upward flow of air as the aircraft descends keeps the rotor turning. It now effectively acts as a parachute and also stores energy which can be used to slow the descent immediately before landing. All helicopters must demonstrate this capability before being awarded a type certificate. The highest altitude from which a helicopter has been landed safely with a dead engine is 40,814 feet, so it clearly works....

In the autogyro, the engine drives a propeller which drives the machine forward while an autorotating rotor replaces the wing of a conventional aeroplane and provides the lift. There are occasional rumours that McCandless invented this device, but this is untrue. That honour belongs to one Juan de la Cierva whose machine first flew – successfully at least – in 1923. What is true is that in 1959 Rex and Cromie bought a de Havilland Hornet Moth biplane. Rex, the problem-solving engineer, could see limitations in this machine and also ways to overcome them and this was when he built the 'McCandless Autogyro'. As befits a motorcycle racer he tested it himself, of course!

In 1943 the McCandless brothers had started their own business on Dublin Road, Belfast, and taken on general engineering work. The workmanship was of a high standard and they received contracts from the Northern Ireland Ministry of Agriculture. Success and expansion led to a partnership with Artie Bell, under the name Bell and McCandless.

During the 1940s Rex and Cromie worked to develop a racing motorcycle with a frame of Rex's own design. This machine, which they called 'The Benial' (Irish for 'Beast'), had a double loop frame and a swinging arm rear using shock absorbers from a car. The Beast handled so well that before long Rex was selling rear suspension conversion kits to racers of rigid framed bikes and building a reputation which reached well beyond his native land.

By the late 1940s Norton had a problem. Their 'Cammy' engine was excellent but their plunger frames (which had earned the nickname 'garden gates') were not. They handled badly and broke frequently. Joe Craig's efforts to cure these problems by adding material had only made them heavier.

As Norton struggled with their unwieldy, ill-handling and fragile chassis in England, McCandless made contact with Norton's managing director, Gilbert Smith, and told him, 'You are not Unapproachable, and you are not the world's best roadholder. I have

Simon Smith's early 'Garden Gate' Norton. Imagining the sound of that pipe? It's far, far better!

a bicycle which is miles better!' A test was arranged on the Isle of Man – where the Chief Constable was related to Cromie's wife – with Geoff Duke riding the plunger machine and Artie Bell on the McCandless. The rest, as they say, is history. The top brass from Norton stood at Kate's cottage, near the end of the Mountain section of the course, and waited to see which bike was better. Duke, who was the acknowledged master of the course, came through on the limit on his Norton-framed bike, and Bell passed him on the outside travelling smoothly and visibly faster.

Harold Daniell, one of the leading riders of the day, said that the McCandless machine felt like riding on a feather bed compared with the plunger frame and the name stuck. It is certainly more flattering than 'garden gate'!

Norton's 'Cammy' engine was given a new lease of life and they enjoyed 1-2-3 finishes in both the Junior and Senior TTs of 1950.

The racing featherbed frame consists of two separate components, each very roughly rectangular, and each formed from a single length of Reynolds tubing. The ends of each tube cross over each other at the front and the head bearing tube is then welded to the four protruding ends. The rear wheel is supported by a swinging arm and a pair of spring/shock absorber units and the result is a chassis which provides great strength and rigidity relative to its weight. A patent was applied for in 1949 and granted in 1952.

In fact, these frames were effectively of third-party manufacture since Norton did not have the welding or bending capability to make the racing featherbed themselves. The lightweight Reynolds 531 tubing required sif-bronze welding and Rex McCandless, never a Norton employee, brought his own jig (which still exists) over from Belfast and built the frames required by the works racing team himself. Bending a 531 tube

The engine of Simon Smith's bike breathes in through an Amal T10 RN carb. This 'Remote Needle' design was intended specifically for racing engines and was available with either a single float chamber (as here) or with dual floats.

The clutch is a racing 'dry' type naturally. Note the lock wires. These are a sure indication of a genuine competition history.

Above left: The characteristic 'cross-over' tubes at the steering head of a featherbed frame. The strengthening gusset at lower left would not be needed on a Reynolds 531 racing frame and it marks this one out as a mild steel road model.

Above right: The claim Rex McCandless disputed....

Right below: Advert for Reynolds Butted Tubes. (*Courtesy of Grace's Guide*)

is difficult as, away from the ends, it is thin and liable to split if a conventional tube bender is used.

The 'Manx' Norton is now regarded as legendary and a version of the featherbed frame, admittedly built from much cheaper and more easily worked mild steel, became the basis for later versions (1951 Model 88 onwards) of the 'Dominator' road bike.

These later mild steel frames for road use were welded more conventionally using steel filler rod. Even so, welding motorcycle frames remains a job for the experienced.

There were two versions of the featherbed for road use. In its original form the frame was quite wide at the top and many riders found it uncomfortable sitting with knees that far apart. In the 'slimline' version the top tubes are closer together. This also makes the frame slightly lighter, but possibly also slightly less stiff.

Later, during the 1950s, Rex also designed and built racing cars. The McCandless trials car finished third in the 1956 Boxing Day Trial, and for 1953 there were a pair of remarkable 500cc Norton-engined circuit racers with fully enclosed bodywork and an ingenious four-wheel-drive system. A chain took drive to the gearbox, then a second drove the front axle. From here a third chain transferred power to the centre of the car where the car's twin drum brakes were located and one more chain then drove the rear wheels. It can be argued that the extra weight and mechanical complexity would have more than balanced out the traction gained by driving all four wheels, since the small engine was not producing a great deal of power to begin with. Nevertheless, the machines attracted attention and achieved good results, especially in hill-climb events, in the hands of both Rex himself and Laurie McGladery.

The cars attracted the attention of Harry Ferguson who provided funding for further development. The British Army also expressed an interest and at one point Rex was apparently offered the Technical Directorship of Harry Ferguson Limited, but declined it.

Ferguson are, of course, famed for their tractors and other agricultural equipment, but they also went on to do a great deal of work on four-wheel drive. The Ferguson P99 of 1961 was not only the first 4WD Formula One car, but also the last front-engined car to win a Formula One race. Many other manufacturers in Formula One and a few in American Indy racing followed the 4WD route in the following decade, although more conventional mid-engined, rear-wheel-drive designs eventually won the day.

It is interesting to note at this point how a machine which performs well on the road can be found wanting under the extreme stresses of racing. Simon Smith, owner of a truly superb-sounding 1947 garden gate machine, has told this author that it handles extremely well under road conditions and has given no problems of breakage. When asked where the problems were under race conditions he pointed out weaknesses at the rear around the plunger itself, but added that the gearbox mounting and the head-stock area had all been known to break – so that would be the front, the middle and the back then! Otherwise the frame was safe. He admitted, perhaps ironically, that the race riders probably knew it was broken when it really started to handle to their liking....

So revolutionary was the featherbed that it quickly became the basis for a raft of

David Hailwood
displaying a
rather tasty
'Norvin' hybrid at
Mallory Park in
2010. (*Courtesy
of Ron Coombs*)

hybrid machines during the era of the 'café racer'. A variety of different engines could be fitted. Hence, with a Triumph engine we have the 'Triton'. Rarer featherbed-based specials even include the 'NorVin' with a mighty Vincent V-twin powerplant. As the Vincent engine was capable of acting as a stressed member, the lower tubes of the Norton frame were sometimes removed.

The Woden is a bit special. This beautiful one-off is based on a 1953 Manx (ie., genuine Reynolds 531) Featherbed frame and fitted with a 500cc JAP V-twin. I have seen a claim that it was built by ex-Brooklands sprinter Francis Williams in the late 1950s or early 1960s, and that it was raced in the Senior TT in 1969 by Steve Woods. Unfortunately I have found no independent record of this, but if correct it would most likely make the Woden the last all-British V-twin bike to race in the event.

Featherbed frames are still available new as several specialist manufacturers produce them from the original specification. This explains the name 'Unity' seen on the tank

Above: The Norton F1 road bike has a Wankel rotary engine and lots of really cool bits such as fork yokes machined from solid billet alloy.

Above: Arlette Chardin of the French Triton Club rode this machine from Paris to the Isle of Man for the 2012 Manx Grand Prix meeting. Along with husband Andre and other Club members she believes that classic motorcycles ought to be ridden.

Right: Andre Chardin's equally well-ridden Triton.

Opposite left: When the featherbed-based Dominator was finally replaced in 1967, Norton made the surprising decision to retain a pre-unit engine/gearbox layout. The engine of the new Commando model was inclined forward and fitted on 'isolastic' mountings to reduce vibration. The Commando was a major success, remaining in production for a decade, with the 'Interpol' variant being supplied in large numbers to police forces worldwide.

A very neat Triton spotted at the roadside.

of one of the hybrids pictured. Unity Equipe, based in Todmorden, near Rochdale, describe themselves as 'Manx Norton, Triumph and Triton specialists'. These bikes look superb and it may be expected that with modern brakes etc. they are even better than the originals.

It is well known, via magazine and television exposure, that these café racers are popular in the United States, but the enthusiasm for British bikes also exists in many other parts of the world. There is, for example, a thriving Triton club in France. They do not restrict themselves to Tritons as such, but most ride either Triumph or Norton machines. Other British makes, such as Velocette and BSA, are tolerated, and when I spent some time with them in 2012 there was one couple present with a *Kawasaki*, but it was disguised with a non-standard colour scheme and no tank badges!

The group includes riders of many different ages and levels of experience and places a high importance on actually riding the machines. They do not believe in 'concours condition' (to use a French term) or transporting the bikes on trailers; they prefer to ride to events. They did have a small support van for tools and spares, but considering that they live all over France and that this is a large country, many habitually ride seriously long distances. Two of the leading lights are husband and wife Andre (known as DeDe) and Arlette Chardin. Both own genuine Tritons and Arlette also owns a chopper with a big springer fork. She can give lessons in kick-starting Speed Twin engines as required.

It is noticeable that when a large number of old British bikes are together in one place, there are always one or two partially dismantled, but then the owners don't

These two were waiting to be photographed in a car park.

just enjoy riding classic bikes for a hobby, they also get pleasure from tinkering with them.

Café Racers

The 1950s and '60s saw the development of a phenomenon known as the café racer. This was the era of Rock 'n' Roll. It was also a time, soon after the war, in which the teenager was becoming a recognised group in society.

Teenagers had money to spend but cars were too expensive. Motorbikes offered an unbeatable combination of excitement and rebellion at a price that many could afford. The practical requirement to wear leather only added to the desired image – especially if the leather was decorated with badges and slogans.

Rock 'n' Roll music was not played by radio stations in its early days; if you wanted to hear it you needed to go out to somewhere like a café with a Juke Box. The term 'café racer' stems from the practice (illegal and dangerous, of course, and therefore highly attractive) of racing from 'café to café' or from 'café to roundabout and back'. The races were often linked directly to the music. Put a coin in the Juke Box and ride to the agreed point and back before the music stopped. Few records of the period lasted longer than three minutes and many were shorter. If the rider could achieve the 'ton' (100 mph) at some point along the route he was seen as belonging to the elite. Some British Rock and Roll bands, such as Johnny Kidd and the Pirates, owed much of their rise to these cafés.

There were to be several British racers who gained a taste for speed on the roads, among them Dave Degens (according to the Ace Café website). Phil Read has said that he took to racing on circuits as he felt he was safer there, with marshals on hand round every corner – and of course there is no oncoming traffic.

It needs to be realised that simply reaching 100 mph was far more difficult on the bikes of the period (and on the roads of the period) than on a modern superbike with its massive power, excellent handling and superb brakes. Only the faster machines then could reach the magic ton and stopping was not too easy either. Accidents and fatalities were fairly frequent and the police, not to mention the wider public and even the older and more conventional motorcyclists, took an understandably dim view of the whole thing.

The bikes used were many and varied. Essentially any proper motorbike was allowed with 'proper' effectively meaning 'not a scooter', since these were the preserve of the despised mods, a fashion-conscious teen group who would not be seen in scuffed leather....

Riders were keen to customise their bikes, both to make them distinctive and faster. There were racer-style features, such as low handlebars (known as clip-ons, since they are clamped separately to the fork tubes rather than running across the top of the yoke), tuned engines, loud exhausts; these add-ons and many others were common and produced a look which can clearly be seen as the precursor of the road-going superbike.

A modern re-enactment of the café racer craze is active in many places today, especially the USA, where restored or replica British bikes are in demand. Often these modern-day café bikes are fitted with exotic engines, such as Guzzi V-twins, which few British riders of the 1960s could possibly have afforded, but the style of the bikes is retained and this author has no doubt that the original café bikers would have been more than happy with them. Certainly the ton no longer poses a problem.

One of the most famous British biker cafés still exists. The Ace Café originally opened in 1938 just off the North Circular Road in London, and although the original building was destroyed in a German raid on the nearby Willesden railway marshalling yard during the Second World War, the café was rebuilt in 1949 and the current building is therefore the one the rockers of the 1950s and '60s knew. It closed in 1969 as fashions changed and a new generation of teenagers chose different ways to express themselves, but a reunion event in 1994 attracted a claimed 12,000 people with even greater numbers in succeeding years when the 'Ace Days' were held in Brighton since the actual café site couldn't accommodate the crowds. Given the popularity of such celebrations it is hardly surprising that the Ace reopened in 1997. It is now regarded as something of a Mecca for bikers who gather to mull over old times, listen to live music, watch stunt shows and even buy food and drink from the café. Nowadays scooters are allowed too. Car drivers now see it as a more general haven for petrolheads. Let's face it; most old bikers now own cars as well. TV shows such as Top Gear and Fifth Gear have filmed at the Ace and it has featured in more than one movie.

Chapter 11

The Independent Builders

Colin Seeley

One of the great motorcycle frame designers, Colin Seeley, was born in January 1936. His father was an enthusiastic biker who rode a Triumph until he could save enough to buy a Vincent, so Colin's interest in motorbikes is perhaps hardly surprising. He began riding and racing in his youth and quickly specialised in sidecar driving.

Between the years 1961 and 1967 Seeley achieved a great deal of success, winning the 1964 Dutch Grand Prix and setting new lap and race records on the way. He came close to winning the World Sidecar Championship on his Dunstall-engined outfit, finishing third in 1964 and 1966 – at a time when the BMW-powered partnerships of Deubel/Horner and Scheidegger/Robinson were dominant – and finishing second in the 1964 Isle of Man Sidecar TT, a race in which he competed seven times, finishing all but once and collecting six silver replicas.

Seeley retired from racing to concentrate on building and preparing machines using his own frames when AMC became bankrupt in 1966. AMC were bought by Manganese Bronze Holdings who formed a new company to be called Norton-Villiers, but since only the Norton road bike component of the company was profitable, Seeley was able to buy the AMC racing department and the rights to the Manx Norton design and spares. The deal included the tooling needed to continue manufacture of the AJS/Matchless G50 engine and he thus secured a supply of engines for his own frames.

The resulting Seeley G50 was set to become one of the most successful machines of its generation with, among many other achievements, wins in the 1968 and 1969 British Championship for Dave Croxford, plus a win for John Cooper at the North West 200, one of the world's most prestigious road races. No less than four Seeley machines finished in the top ten in the 1969 Senior TT. Even these results were eclipsed when privateer Tommy Robb rode a G50 to fourth place in the 1970 500cc World Championship. This was the predecessor of the MotoGP World Championship of today.

Seeley eventually produced four versions of his racing frame (Marks I-IV), the later versions being adapted to the Norton Commando engine. As the British engines were eventually overtaken – literally – in the 1970s by the Japanese, Seeley produced frames to fit Honda motorcycle engines and even for competition cars as well.

A pair of Seeley-framed machines are effective studies in elegant design. The bike in the foreground carries a Norton engine; the other is a Yamaha-engined 'Yamsel'.

There was also a short-lived road version of the G50 that sold under the name 'Seeley Condor'. This used the G50 engine suspended from a beautiful lightweight frame with no front downtubes. The major problems in constructing this bike lay in providing power for the road-bike electrics, since the race engine had no provision to generate power for lighting. Replicas of the Condor are still available from TT winner Steve Tonkin. These attractive bikes are constructed around frames built by Roger Titchmarsh and fitted with George Beale engines. The Tonkin Typhoon uses a G50 engine but Steve also offers the Tempest model with a BSA single; the Tornado is a Manx Norton replica. Of course, all the names spell TT….

Barry Sheene turned to Seeley in 1971 when looking for a good frame for his Suzuki T500 engine. The result was a bronze-welded Reynolds 531 beauty on which he won the British Championship and which he said was 'the best handling bike I ever rode'.

In 1973, Seeley entered into a partnership with Bernie Ecclestone. At that time Ecclestone was principal of the Brabham Formula One team and Formula One cars had been using monocoque chassis since Colin Chapman designed his Lotus 25 for the 1962 season. The monocoque was stiffer than the tubular spaceframes it rendered obsolete, and also much lighter. These have long been the twin desires of structural engineers, yet motorcycle frames continued to be formed from welded tubes.

Seeley and Ecclestone planned to bring the advantages of the monocoque to bear on Grand Prix motorcycle design, combining Seeley's motorcycle-building experience and Brabham's fabrication facilities.

Oddly, Brabham had been one of the last constructors to hold out against monocoque construction in Formula One. Long-time chief designer Ron Tauranac felt that a well-designed spaceframe was almost as stiff as a monocoque and much easier to repair after an accident. This latter point was particularly important as Brabham supplied 'customer cars' to buyers in various classes of motorsport. However, by 1970, rule changes in Formula One had forced the introduction of monocoque designs.

The bike was powered by a Suzuki 500cc engine, as by this time Japanese two-strokes had rendered the earlier British four-strokes uncompetitive.

The bike's early outings seemed to show promise. In its first race at Mallory Park, Sheene almost won. He was only prevented when a piece of lining material came loose in the fuel tank and blocked the outlet moments from the end. On this occasion, however, Sheene was apparently unimpressed by the new machine's handling. He was later reported to have described the bike as 'a bag of s---'.

It is interesting to note that more recent efforts to introduce carbon fibre frames into MotoGP (again seeking increased stiffness and reduced weight) have led to riders complaining that the bikes are difficult to ride. It has become accepted that some limited flex is actually desirable in a road racing frame.

The relationship between Ecclestone and Seeley did not go well as the season progressed, and the project eventually collapsed. The Seeley monocoque became a museum piece; one of the many 'almost successful' machines with which motorsport history is sadly littered.

Not all 'Seeley' machines have actually been built by Seeley himself. Just as Colin Seeley continued to develop and manufacture the Matchless/AJS G50, so others have continued to build Seeley G50s. The best-known names associated with the more modern bikes are those of Fred Walmsley, George Beale and Roger Titchmarsh.

Fred Walmsley, George Beale and Roger Titchmarsh

Walmsley is based in Preston, Lancashire, and offers a full range of services on Manx, G50 and 7R machinery. Whether it be race preparation, rebuilding or a complete bike built from scratch and to order, Walmsley has a superb reputation.

Roger Titchmarsh is a noted frame builder specialising in 531 frames for bikes such as the Manx Norton and Seeley Matchless. Several Manx Grand Prix races have been won by riders using Titchmarsh frames and his son Dan has followed him into the same line of work, setting up his own business offering a range of motorcycle design and engineering work.

George Beale has been manufacturing parts for the Matchless G50 and AJS 7R since 1971 and sponsoring racers for almost as long. After moving up to Grand Prix level in 1978, Beale became the largest privateer entrant in Europe, with a team of riders including such names as Roger Marshall and Mick Grant. His stated ambition to win a TT was finally realised in 1984 when Australian rider Graeme McGregor won the Junior race on one of Dr Joe Ehrlich's 250cc Rotax-engined EMC machines. This was effectively a factory bike but Beale owned and ran the team. McGregor then went on to win the Formula 2 race later the same day.

From 1989 Beale began to build up a restoration business providing a much-needed service to owners of all types of classic motorcycles. This led naturally to the construction of complete machines early in the 1990s, and the first were G50 and 7R replicas, although these were eventually joined by 350cc and 500cc Benelli four-cylinder bikes.

During the 1990s Beale-built Matchless G50s became the dominant force in the American Classic Championship, winning numerous times – including seven straight victories in the Classic '60s race at Daytona.

Paul Dunstall

Paul Dunstall entered his father's business selling mopeds and scooters soon after leaving school. He also began racing motorcycles in the late 1950s, at the age of 18, using a 600cc Norton Dominator which he converted to race specification, fitting – and in many cases making – new parts himself.

Although achieving enough success to prove that the converted Dominator was a quick bike, able to take on and beat many of the conventional race bikes of the day, Paul only raced for a couple of years, deciding that the engineering side gave him greater satisfaction.

A racing friend, Fred Neville, asked him to build a Dominator for him to race, and the Dunstall reputation began to grow. Having designed a pair of swept back exhausts to allow a slimmer fairing to be fitted, he displayed them in the scooter shop and soon received more than fifty orders!

The pipes were soon followed by clip-on bars, headlamp brackets, both alloy and glass-fibre fuel tanks and rearset footrests. The first Dunstall catalogue was printed in 1961 and the business was established.

The next part of the Dunstall story bears a striking similarity to that of Colin Seeley. Like Seeley, Dunstall took a risk in order to progress. In 1962 AMC closed the Norton plant in Birmingham and consolidated Norton and Matchless production. Dunstall bought the racing Dominator engines (known as 'Domiracers') and parts, which had been under development for the Norton factory race team. The sale included a complete bike which had been ridden to third place in the 1961 Senior TT. In fact the original works rider, Tom Phillips, joined Neville as a Dunstall-entered rider for a time during the 1963 season.

Tragedy sometimes strikes in motorcycle racing, and Fred Neville was killed riding an AJS 7R in wet conditions during the Senior Manx Grand Prix of 1961. He was in the lead by over two minutes on the last lap, but lost control at Greeba Bridge, an extremely fast left hand bend with a slight hump on the exit.

Dunstall had been impressed by a keen 23-year-old rider named Dave Downer and signed him for the following season. Downer sadly also died, while dicing for the lead at Brands Hatch in 1963, and Manxman Syd Mizen took over as Dunstall's rider. In fact, over the next few years a remarkable number of Britain's top racers rode for Dunstall. The list would include Joe Dunphy, Derek Minter, Peter Williams,

A rare, and also sadly poignant picture of Dave Downer on the Dunstall Dominator shortly before his accident. (*Courtesy of Ron Coombs*)

Ray Pickrell and Dave Degens. Colin Seeley also used both 650cc and 750cc Dunstall Domiracer engines in his sidecar outfits.

Meantime, Paul was developing a road version of the Domiracer and also took on the Norton agency while sales of scooters and mopeds slumped in the early 1960s, almost failing completely by the end of 1964. Dunstall moved away from his original business and in 1966 he began to supply complete motorcycles using his own parts. He had developed many modified and new parts for Norton engines and others so that by this time he was able to give customers the opportunity to determine the exact specifications. He offered machines based on the BSA 500cc and 650cc twins, Norton 650cc and 750cc models, and the Triumph 500cc and 650cc machines. This proved to be good business. Within two years 300 fully customised bikes were sold.

Meanwhile, trouble was brewing on the production class racing scene as some began to question whether the Dunstall racers were 'standard' as required by the rules. Such controversies are virtually inevitable in motorsport whenever a standard or 'production' class is devised. Not all factory-produced machines are identical; they are manufactured to specified tolerances, which may allow quite significant variations. On the road these don't matter, but in racing they do – especially if an engine is dismantled and all components either replaced or machined to the optimal sizes allowed within the maker's tolerances. Such 'blueprinting' as it is known may make a big difference to the engine's performance, but since all components are individually legal the engine must still be accepted. If the original manufacturer varies the specifications during a production run (as often happens) the situation becomes still more complicated. Can you mix parts from early and late models? If not, can the organisers hope to police it? Of course, blueprinting is extremely expensive and production classes are often intended to provide relatively low-cost racing; hence the arguments.

Clearly Paul Dunstall's special parts were not standard Norton, BSA or Triumph, but the UK tax authorities had classified Dunstall Motorcycles as a manufacturer in its own right – and the ACU had homologated the Dunstall Dominators as legal machines for the 1967 Production TT. Dunstall was able to demonstrate that his factory machines were essentially the same as his road bikes when speed trap measurements were made on the Isle of Man. The factory Dominator reached 132 mph and a stock bike recorded just short of 130 mph.

By 1968 the Dunstall business was international, with important markets in the USA and Sweden. The Dunstall American model was introduced, with high level handlebars and exhausts and a twin leading shoe drum brake instead of the twin discs fitted to British bikes. It was not actually available to buy in America though and customers had to buy one and ship it out, with all the resulting additional costs. Not until 1973 was it possible to begin shipping machines directly to US dealers.

1968 was significant not only for the introduction of the 'American' but also for the first appearance in Paul's range of parts for Japanese motorcycles.

Alf Hagon

Alf Hagon has his surname on many of the best maintained classic machines. As a rider, starting from the age of 18 in 1950, Hagon had a 12-year Speedway career and became British grass-track champion no less than eleven times. While riding in grasstrack events on BSA specials powered by JAP engines he felt strongly that the bikes were too heavy; with support from sponsor Tom Kirby, he built a lightweight sprung frame to fit the 350cc JAP motor. These 'Kirby Specials' were enormously successful and Hagon won races on them for more than a decade. He also competed with outstanding success in drag racing, making the first sub-ten second pass by a British rider in the summer of 1967.

Along the way Hagon found time to start a business. In 1958 he began building speedway and grass-track frames in his mother's small garden shed, but within two years Hagon Products occupied premises at 350-352 High Road in Leyton East London and Alf was living above the shop. Frames made there have won numerous world championships and when the Pentonville Wheel Works was acquired in 1965, the firm began to build and repair wheels.

Today the Hagon name is associated strongly with shock absorbers. Girling Shock Absorbers were one of the main suppliers to the Hagon frame building business and when they ceased production in 1985, Hagon bought the tooling for the entire range. A visit to the company web site today will reveal that Hagon, now run by Alf's son Martin, can supply new shocks, wheels or fork springs for almost any machine from a 1957 James Colonel to a Velocette Thruxton.

Dennis Jones

The remarkable Dennis Jones was born in 1916 in Draycott, Derbyshire, and served an engineering apprenticeship at Rolls Royce during the 1930s, working in the aero engine department under Lord Ernest Hives who led the development of the Merlin engine among others.

During the Second World War, Jones was involved in the development of the Motor Torpedo Boats (MTBs) powered by a marine variant of the Merlin, which later took part in the important St Nazaire Raid. He also had the privilege of working for a time with Sir Frank Whittle, the inventor of the jet engine, and in later life he was a founding partner of Cue and Jones who, at the time, were suppliers of invalid carriages to the Ministry of Pensions.

He had actually begun racing motorcycles just before the Second World War on his JAP-engined OK-Supreme. It was perhaps inevitable that, as an engineer, he would soon be making modifications and improvements to racing machines, but Dennis Jones went much further than this.

Soon after the war ended he set about designing a supercharged flat four two-stroke engine and built it himself, in his spare time, in a workshop at his home. An engine needs a chassis so he built that too – not just the frame with its plunger rear end, but the forks and the brakes as well. Almost as soon as the bike was completed, supercharging was banned from motorcycle racing and it was therefore not eligible to race. Most people would have been discouraged at this point, but in 1947 Jones started building his second bike. This time he designed an air-cooled four-stroke 250cc twin with double overhead camshafts, fitted it into a double cradle frame and raced it with some success, although this was limited by unreliability. The problem was persistent as big ends and connecting rods failed repeatedly.

The twin had worked well enough to impress Ernest Earles (designer of the Earles fork detailed elsewhere in this book) and a partnership with Earles and the well-known rider Bill Lomas resulted in another 250cc twin, which Lomas planned to ride at the 1955 TT. In the event, however, MV made him one of those offers no racer can refuse.

Jones next built a four-cylinder 500cc machine. The engine was effectively two of his twins on a single crankshaft, but of course he still had to make the components himself. This time he even made his own carburettors although he allowed himself to fit a pair of Norton forks! A number of good riders raced 'Jones Specials' and the designer himself achieved numerous awards, including replicas on the Isle of Man. When asked how he could achieve the things he did, he replied that anyone could do it....

Dave Degens

Dave Degens was a successful racer of the 1960s who was perhaps never as famous as he ought to have been. He began to build frames under the name Dresda at the time when the Japanese were putting the large, established British bike makers such as Norton and Triumph under serious financial pressure. Some would argue that the quality of British

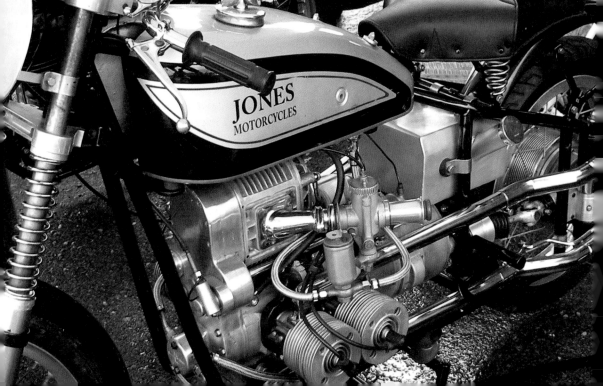

machines dropped at this time as corners were cut in order to reduce costs. Possibly the Japanese bikes simply 'showed up' faults which had always been there, such as oil leaks from vertically split crankcases. Whichever version is true – and the answer is probably 'a bit of both' – it cannot be denied that the supply of original featherbed frames began to dry up and a gap appeared in the market for the smaller builder.

Degens began with featherbed based designs for Tritons, but he moved on with the times and embraced the Japanese engines too. So successful was he that, having won the Barcelona 24-hour race twice (in 1965 and 1970) with Triumph engined machines, he was approached by the French company Japauto with a request to build an endurance racing bike around a Honda four-cylinder engine. This resulted in a pair of wins in 1972 and 1973 for a 969cc Honda with a Dresda frame in the world famous Bol D'Or.

On one occasion, following one of his Barcelona wins, he was supplied with a 750cc twin engine by Yamaha, who were looking to get into endurance racing, and commissioned to build a chassis for it. The engine had a lot of problems and did not run well at all, so Degens took it apart and made a number of modifications which improved things considerably. According to an interview he gave some years ago, Yamaha were impressed. They told him that the official development work was being done by Porsche in Germany and asked him to go over there and help.

He found the Porsche version of the engine running extremely badly on a very high tech and expensive test bed, but on examining it he saw that they had assembled the Amal carburettors with the throttle slides in back to front! He didn't tell them what the problem was, but simply refitted the slides correctly and amazed the white-coated technicians with the sudden improvement in the behaviour of their engine.

The business is still thriving and producing not only Tritons to order but various other 'specials' as well. The Dresda website gives information on recent projects including bikes based on AJS, Vincent, BSA and JAP engines.

Harris Performance Products Ltd

Harris Performance Products Ltd was established in the 1970s by brothers Steve and Lester Harris and additional director Stephen Bayford; the company has a strong commitment to motorcycle sport. This enthusiast approach has continued to the present day and the firm's website states that they are 'great supporters of the adage "racing improves the breed"'.

The company has enjoyed racing success in World Superbikes, Grand Prix racing and the Isle of Man TT, and in 1991 Harris became one of only two companies licensed to buy Yamaha race engines for the construction of 500cc Grand Prix machines based on a non-Yamaha chassis.

Harris were also the chassis partner for the 2003 Sauber Petronas MotoGP project. Although this never made it to the GP grid, a homologation run of 150 were built

Opposite above and below: Two of Dennis Jones' truly amazing hand-made motorcycles, the 500cc dohc and the supercharged two-stroke. Anyone could do it? (*Courtesy of Ron Coombs*)

with an 899.5cc version of the (originally 989cc) three-cylinder inline engine to meet the rules of the Superbike World Championship.

Petronas joined forces with Carl Fogarty to run the bikes, but unfortunately for them the FIM rules changed to allow 1,000cc machines. The Foggy Petronas entries, built under the old rules, were therefore at a major disadvantage but they still managed a couple of podium finishes in 2004.

In addition to the various racing programmes Harris have, over the last 40-plus years they have built a total of more than 2,200 road bikes, including the Harris Magnum series, based on their own frame designs. Although most of the bikes have engines made in other parts of the world, Harris frames continue the tradition of British chassis design which is as old as motorcycling itself.

Rickman Metisse

In scrambling/motocross circles the Rickman Metisse name borders on legendary. In the 1950s and '60s, Don and Derek Rickman were right up there as riders alongside the likes of Jeff Smith and Arthur Lampkin – himself the first of a continuing dynasty of great trials champions – and in 1957 they began to supply parts for scrambles machines.

In 1961 they began to produce their own frames, and initially considered calling them 'Mongrels' since they worked to the philosophy that there were good frames and good engines but that somebody needed to combine the two. Obviously this wouldn't have sounded too good so they looked for a classier alternative and came up with the French feminine adjective Metisse. It is often said that this just means mongrel, but in reality it avoids the negative undertones of the English word and has no perfect English equivalent.

The Rickman Metisse frame is based on the requirement for extreme stiffness. The front and rear wheels must not twist relative to each other. To this end the head bearing tube is supported not only by four cross-over tubes as in the Norton Featherbed but by two additional braces; six tubes in all. It is made from Reynolds 531 tubing and is also very light and saved further weight by carrying the oil within the frame tubes. The bare frame typically weighs less than 23 lbs (or just over 10 kg). Various additional parts, including the fuel tank and seat, were made of fibreglass.

One significant source of flex in a conventional frame is the swinging arm at the rear since it must allow for easy and quick adjustment of the chain. This is normally provided by moving the wheel spindle fore and aft and locking it in position, but this method reduces the torsional stiffness of the two sides of the arm.

The Rickmans tackled this by welding tubular sleeves for the spindle in fixed positions at the ends of the swinging arm and providing chain adjustment at the forward end by allowing repositioning of the arm pivot. The frame lugs carry elongated slots for the pivot bar and additional circular discs are fitted to locate the pivot bar within these slots. Each frame was supplied with ten pairs of discs, each positioning the swinging arm $^{1}/_{32}$ inch further towards the rear.

At a time when virtually all scramblers were using single-cylinder engines, the Rickman brothers chose to fit the Triumph Tiger 100 and the 'mongrel' – sorry 'Metisse' – was completed by using Norton forks. The customer frames could be supplied with engine mountings, made of Duralumin (Dural) for lightness, to fit Triumph or AMC singles, plus BSA or AMC gearboxes. A smaller version of the frame with a single front downtube, the Petite-Metisse, was designed to fit a Bultaco engine.

Spondon Engineering Ltd

Spondon Engineering Ltd are frame specialists and take their name from their home town of Spondon, near Derby. Spondon have produced frames for a vast range of engines and are considered to be one of the top British frame makers. The current big tube 'Monster' frame fits engines such as the Yamaha R1 and Suzuki GSX and gives a real 'streetfighter' feel.

Founded by Bob Stevenson and Stuart Tiller in 1969, the company is now owned by Stuart Garner, who also owns the Norton name; the Norton that caused such a stir on the Isle of Man in 2012 when it arrived for the Senior TT carried its Aprilia engine in a Spondon frame. This was not the first time the Spondon and Norton names had been linked, though. The rotary-engined and JPS sponsored RCW 588 racer, which was setting so many records in the 1989 season and spawned the F1 Sport road bike, used a Spondon twin-spar frame.

Spondon-framed Yamaha racer. The general layout is similar to the much earlier Seeley, but alloy box sections replace 531 tube for greatly increased stiffness. Times change.

Selected Glossary of Mechanical Innovations

Amal Carburettors

Amal carburettors were made from the 1920s and are still available new today as the current owners of the name (Burlen Fuel Systems Ltd) have a major commitment to supplying parts for classic British machinery. The name itself may relate to the 'amal'gamation of several different companies in the years following the First World War.

What is certain is that Amal carbs established a great reputation as essentially simple, yet solid designs that functioned well and were easily worked on by their owners. Many of the developments made over the years were aimed at reducing manufacturing costs by further increasing this inherent simplicity.

The earliest models – known as the 'Standard' series – used float chambers which were separate from the main body and this arrangement continued on the 'TT' and 'GP' models intended for high performance and racing engines. The float chamber could be mounted rigidly to the main body or remotely.

In 1954 the company introduced the 'Monobloc' carb. As its name indicates, this has the float chamber incorporated in the main body although it is set to one side of the throttle and jet assembly. The picture on p. 147 shows a Monobloc carburettor fitted to a BSA C15.

The 'Concentric' design made its appearance in 1967 and is a masterpiece of neatness and simplicity. The float is now vertically beneath the throttle slide and concentric with it. There was little to go wrong and in any case the carburettor could be removed from the bike, stripped, cleaned and reassembled in next to no time – even by an inexperienced teenage mechanic such as the author then was! A brilliant little carburettor which was manufactured (as all the previous models had been) in a range of sizes to fit the requirements of different engines.

The Concentric range was developed over time through Mark 1 (Zinc alloy body, cold starting by both air slide and a 'tickler' to flood the float bowl), Mark 1.5 (cold starting system with its own petrol and air supplies) and Mark 2 (aluminium body) versions and declined in popularity only as a result of the decline in British motorcycle manufacturing.

Epicyclic Gears

An epicyclic (or planetary) gearbox provides smooth, quiet and efficient transfer of rotation between concentric shafts and allows three modes of operation, two of which give 'forward' gear ratios. These compact and elegant mechanisms are not new; such gearings were known to the ancient Greeks, as can be seen in the remarkable 'antikythera device', constructed by hand, long before the days of machine tools, to allow precise astronomical calculations (for more information see the website www.antikythera-mechanism.gr).

Differential gears work on very similar lines, but for a totally modern application of planetary gears you need look no further than the Toyota Prius. Its 'Power Split Device', which divides the torque of the internal combustion engine between the road wheels and the motor/generator system is actually an epicyclic gear set. The combustion engine drives the planet frame and the torque is divided between the ring gear and the sun wheel. The ratio is fixed but the power transmitted from the electric and internal combustion motors is continuously variable. A central 'sun' wheel drives a group of 'planets' (usually three or four) attached to a metal frame and these in turn mesh with an outer ring gear toothed on its inner face. When used as a gearbox, the mode of operation is determined by locking the mechanism in one of three ways.

- In star mode, the planet frame is locked in position and the sun and ring gears rotate. This causes the ring to rotate in the opposite direction to the sun wheel and at a slower speed. The ratio is fixed by the number of teeth on the sun and ring, but may be as high as 10:1.
- In planetary mode, the ring gear is fixed and the sun and planet frame rotate. The frame rotates more slowly than the sun wheel, but in the same direction. A ratio up to 12:1 is possible.
- In solar mode, the sun is fixed and the planet frame and ring rotate. The ring moves in the same direction as the frame and at twice the speed.

In all modes the gearbox may give either a reduction or an increase in rotational speed depending on which of the moving components is being driven.

IOE Engines

IOE-type engines were pursued by a number of motorcycle and car manufacturers as they did offer some advantages over a conventional overhead or side-valve configuration. The inlet valve is mounted above the combustion chamber and operated conventionally by a pushrod and rocker (or even by atmospheric pressure in some very early designs) while the exhaust valve is built into the cylinder wall and opened by a cam. This potentially gives good gas flow as it allows larger valves to be used. It also improves cooling of the exhaust valve and spring. In the early narrow bore, long-stroke engines the larger valves were particularly desirable.

Early Land Rovers used a version of the Rover IOE engine as it was able to use poor quality petrol. Its angled block surface and pitched-roof pistons allowed the inlet valve to run very close to the piston top and this gave good 'squish' to the combustion chamber, allowing high compression without detonation. This engine remained available as an option until 1980.

The Kliktronic System

Kliktronic have been producing specialised gear changing systems for bikes (and the increasingly popular bike-engined track cars) since 1997. The Kliktronic system was designed by Bob Sirett and Keith Holland in response to the needs of Bob's son Carl, who had been injured in a motorcycle accident. Carl wished to resume riding but was unable to operate a conventional foot-operated gear lever.

The pair produced an electronic shifter which enables shifts at the press of a button on the handlebar. It is even sensitive enough to enable neutral to be selected when required. The clutch is needed for moving off and for downshifts – although the makers claim that some gearboxes will allow clutchless downshifts if the rider is sufficiently skilful in matching revs.

Although it has proved its usefulness to disabled riders, the system sells to others too as its fast action (particularly when used in conjunction with an ignition interrupt device) also makes it useful for track work.

The Reynolds Tube

John Reynolds began manufacturing nails in Birmingham in 1841, but in 1897 the company invented – and patented – the process which would establish the Reynolds name as a byword for excellence in both engineering and wheeled sport. It was a process for producing tubes which were thicker at the ends than in the middle, yet had a constant external diameter; its significance was that it enabled bicycle manufacturers to build frames which were both strong and light. Prior to this, reinforcing butted joints meant using thicker tube or adding metal – either gussets or inserts within the tube ends. Using the Reynolds tube the builder could now use thin tube and make strong joints without additional metal pieces.

A separate offshoot of the firm, The Patent Butted Tube Company Ltd, was established in 1898. This was renamed Reynolds Tube Company Ltd in 1923 and became TI Reynolds 531 Ltd, following a takeover by Tube Investments Ltd, but they have never left Birmingham. In fact, following the bankruptcy of then-owners Coyote Sports, a management buyout was organised successfully in 2000 to keep Reynolds in their home city.

As early as 1902 they produced their first catalogue of cycle tubing and the top of the range set weighed only 4½ lbs (just over 2 kg). If you wanted to produce a lightweight bicycle it had to be made using a Reynolds tube set. Note that tubes are supplied in sets since each tube must be butted at its ends in manufacture so you can't just buy a length and cut pieces as required.

The First World War brought not only large contracts to supply tubing for both bicycles and motorcycles, but also for the 'new thing' – aircraft. The company's connection with the aerospace industry continues to the present day, and during the war years, the factory expanded so much that new and larger premises were needed, and Reynolds moved to what would be their home for the next 90 years at Hay Hall. The present factory is only a mile away in Hall Green.

As peace returned, further diversification took them into the car industry as well. In peacetime Reynolds transferred some of the knowledge gained from aircraft back to the needs of cyclists and introduced something possibly as significant as the 'Patent Butted Tube' itself. Their new high manganese (HM) tubing was a genuine improvement over anything previously available, and Reynolds HM Quality tubing remained the world's premier tubing for more than a decade. When it was superseded in 1935 it was only because Reynolds themselves came up with something even better.

Reynolds 531 (pronounced five, three, one rather than the number) is now only available to special order; but it is still available. A manganese molybdenum alloy steel 531 is legendary. Cyclists and motorcyclists have certainly not been the only users. The front and rear frames of the E-Type Jaguar for example were made of 531.

Since 1958 the Tour de France has been won twenty-seven times by riders using Reynolds tube sets and Richard Noble's record-breaking Thrust 2 was actually built using 531 tube at the Reynolds factory.

In the Second World War Reynolds produced 25,000 miles of light alloy tubing for aircraft including the Spitfire and the Blenheim. The workforce at the time was only just over 2,000.

Nowadays, with much of the high volume bicycle making having moved abroad, Reynolds focus on custom-drawn tubes of very high quality which can be found in products such as ice skates, automotive suspension arms, sports wheelchairs, and of course, motorcycles. Their butted X-100 aluminium-lithium tubes were a direct spin-off from work on the NASA space shuttle and Reynolds 953 has a tensile strength twice that of 531. It compares favourably with titanium for some applications.

Sleeve-Valve Engines

Charles Knight had bought an air-cooled three-wheeler in 1901 and been annoyed by its noisy clatter. He set out to design a quieter engine and patented it in 1908. The engine used a pair of cast iron sleeves, with holes in their upper ends, inside each cylinder, with the piston moving inside the inner sleeve. The sleeves moved as the engine rotated and uncovered the inlet and exhaust ports as necessary.

These engines were much quieter than anything previously available and required very little maintenance. They had larger ports than conventional poppet-valved engines, allowing better gas flow. They were also expensive to manufacture due to the accurate machining required and used a lot of oil since it was not possible to fit piston rings and 'running in' made very little difference. Of course, high oil consumption was not unusual at the time since poppet valves were prone to leak badly through the guides, but the higher cost of the Knight engine initially made it hard to sell.

It was Dr Frederick Lanchester (of disc brake fame), working at Daimler, who helped Knight to develop the engine and find a market in luxury vehicles, where the extra cost was acceptable. And from there we get to luxury motorcycles, such as the Grindlay-Peerless.

Further work carried out separately by Peter Burt and James McCollum produced sleeve-valve engines using a combination of reciprocating and rotary sleeve motion and requiring only a single sleeve in each cylinder. The McCollum design placed the sleeve outside the cylinder wall and even outside the water jacket of water-cooled engines. This meant that it was protected from some of the thermal stresses of Burt's engine, but the so-called 'Burt-McCollum' engine built by Barr and Stroud used an internal sleeve and is therefore seen as more 'Burt' than 'McCollum'.

In the end the poppet valve triumphed as better materials, stronger springs, cleaner fuel and more accurate manufacture overcame its weaknesses and the oil-burning problems of the sleeve valve rendered it unable to compete, but nevertheless it has its place in the history of the internal combustion engine.

The Springer Fork

An alternative to the girder fork was the 'springer' in which the fork itself is solid, but the wheel is then carried on a separate pivoted arm, or 'leading link', at the lower end. George Brough used this type of fork on his legendary SS100 and the layout can be clearly seen in the photographs. Springer forks are sometimes seen today on American choppers.

A spring alone is not enough however. The bike will bounce for some distance after passing over a bump in the road unless some form of damping is added. The Manchester-made DOT (whose name means 'Devoid Of Trouble') shows an early solution to this. The fork movement is damped by a pair of friction plates clamped together. Later designs improved on this slightly by providing easier adjustment. The Brough Superior SS100, built in Nottingham, shows how the friction damper was fitted with an elegant and easily operated hand adjuster.

Further Reading and Viewing

Books

Axon, Jo, *Sidecars*, Osprey Publishing, 2008
Belton, Brian, *Fay Taylour: Queen of Speedway*, Panther Publishing Ltd, 2006
Hill, Graham, *Life at the Limit*, Pan Books Ltd, 1969
Jennings, R. L., *To Make a Better Mousetrap: A Biography of Rex McCandless*,
    www.jenningspublishing.co.uk
Jones, Barry, *Granville Bradshaw: A Flawed Genius?*, Panther Publishing, 2008
Lawrence, T. E., *The Mint*, Penguin Modern Classics

Websites

www.antikythera-mechanism.gr
www.bsaownersclub.co.uk
www.dresda.co.uk
www.eahart.com/prius/psd/
www.kliktronic.co.uk
www.sunbeamsidevalve.com

Documentaries

TT Closer to the Edge, CinemaNX Productions Four Limited 2011, Certificate 15

Index